Part Three

FLOOD SUBJECTS

and did, were consciously or otherwise, of great moment to her. After his death the number of elegies she seems to have composed in his memory is a spoken testimony of the veneration she had come to feel for him. There are perhaps as many as six.

Born in 1803, Edward Dickinson was reared on the ideals of the eighteenth century, and helped transmit them to the nineteenth. For him happiness was to be pursued by devotion under God to family and commonwealth, not by declared intent but by resolved action. He was a man of rectitude whose reason governed his passions, and for whom moderation in all things was the rule of life. He met Emily Norcross, the daughter of Joel and Betsey Norcross of Monson, while he was a student at Yale College and Emily was attending a finishing school in New Haven. She had the qualities he knew he wanted in a wife. She was demure, submissive, domestic, and deeply religious. She waited while he went on to complete his law study in his father's office and at the Northampton Law School. Admitted to the bar in August 1826, he raised his sign in September, and a year and a half later, in May 1828, they were married. The letters they exchanged during his courtship survive, and the depth of their affection shines through. He told her he looked forward, not to a life of mere pleasure, but of "rational happiness." In April of the following year William Austin, their first child, was born. Edward Dickinson probably was not intimately acquainted with the poetry of William Wordsworth, nor to be sure did Wordsworth know him, but no portrait of Edward Dickinson more exactly represents him than the "Ode to Duty." He daily listened to the stern daughter of the Voice of God, and lived by her light and law. He had something of his father's sense of dedication to the public weal. In 1835 he became Treasurer of the College, and held that post for thirty-eight years. He not only handled its funds but took charge of its building programs. Except for his hard-headed management, the young institution might well have foundered during the early years.

The conservatism of his disposition was reinforced by the nature of his experiences. Law cases are not won by wishful thinking, nor are buildings erected and railroads chartered by hope alone. He remained all his life a "straight" Whig when the more popular "republican" brand was making headway. His interest in politics was active. Thrice he served in the Massachusetts Legislature, first in 1839, and last in 1874, the year of his death. During the forties he was elected to the State Senate, and served on the Governor's Council. In 1852 he was a delegate to the Baltimore Convention that unsuccessfully sought the nomination of his candidate, Webster, for president. For one term in 1853–1855 he was seated as a Member of Congress. These public activities created rivalries, but the enemies he made were political, not personal. He was forthright, courageous, and trustworthy, a man whom other men respected even when they were not drawn to him personally.

A revealing portrait of Edward Dickinson can be sketched by bringing together many of the references that Emily made to him in her letters written over the years. Because they tell as much about her as about him, they are especially significant. Pulsating between the attraction and repulsion she felt, they are keenly alive to his personality and presence in the house, even after his death. They all derive from letters written to her brother during the years 1851–1854, when he was teaching for a year in Boston, then attending Harvard Law School. Since she is giving Austin a budget of family news in each letter, she would hardly fail to keep him posted on their father.

Father and mother sit in state in the sitting-room perusing such papers, only, as they are well assured, have nothing carnal in them.

Father is as uneasy when you are gone away as if you catch a trout and put him in Sahara.

The meat and potato and a little pan of your favorite brown bread are keeping warm at the fire while father goes for shavings. . . He wore a palm leaf hat and his pantaloons tucked in his boots and I couldn't help thinking of you as he strode along by the window. I don't think negligé quite becoming to so mighty a man.

I wanted to write you Friday, the night of Jennie Lind. . . Father sat all the evening looking *mad* and *silly*, and yet so much amused you would have *died* a-laughing. When the performers bowed, he said "Good evening, sir," and when they retired, "Very well, that will do."

The Kimberly barn burnt down. . . Mr. Palmer's barn took fire, and Deacon Leland's also . . . Father and Mr. Frink took charge of the fire – or rather of the *water*, since fire usually takes care of itself. . . After the whole was over they gave "three cheers for Edward Dickinson," and three more for the insurance company. ·

Father is reading the Bible, I take it for consolation, judging from outward things. . . [His] prayers for you at our morning devotions are enough to break one's heart; it is really very touching.

There was quite an excitement in the village Monday evening. We were all startled by a violent church-bell ringing. . . The sky was a beautiful red, bordering on a crimson and rays of a gold pink color were constantly shooting off from a kind of sun in the centre. . . Father happened to see it among the very first, and rang the bell himself to call attention to it.

He writes [from the Baltimore Convention] that he "should think the whole world was there, and some from other worlds." He says he meets a great many old friends and acquaintances, and forms a great many new ones – he writes in very fine spirits, and says he enjoys himself very much.

Since we have written you the grand railroad decision is made. . . Father is really sober from excessive satisfaction, and bears his honors with a most becoming air.

Father . . . didn't say a word about the Hippodrome or the Museum, and he came home so stern that none of us dared to ask him, and besides grandmother [Norcross] was here, and you certainly don't think I'd allude to a Hippodrome in the presence of that lady! I'd as soon think of popping firecrackers in the presence of Peter the Great.

Your letters are very funny indeed – about the only jokes we have, now you are gone, and I hope you will send us one as often as you can. Father takes great delight in your remarks to him – puts on his spectacles and reads them o'er and o'er as if it was a blessing to have an only son. He reads all the letters you write, as soon as he gets them, at the post-office, no matter to whom addressed . . . and when he gets home in the evening, he cracks a few walnuts, puts his spectacles on, and with your last in his hand, sits down to enjoy the evening. . . I do think it's so funny, you and father do nothing but "fisticuff" all the while you're at home, and the minute you are separated, you become such devoted friends.

Father was, as usual, chief marshall of the day, and went marching around with New London at his heels like some old Roman general upon a triumph day.

We had a very pleasant visit from the Monson folks. They came one noon and stayed till the next. They agree beautifully with father on the "present generation." They decided that they hoped every young man who smoked would take fire. I respectfully intimated that I thought the result would be a vast conflagration, but was instantly put down.

Father . . . gave me quite a trimming about "Uncle Tom" and "Charles Dickens" and these "modern literati" who, he says, are nothing, compared to past generations who flourished when he was a boy.

To Austin she presents the picture of a father they both deeply admire. She is drawn closer to her brother on matters touching upon music and literature because they share an interest in them that is keener than their father's, as they both know. At home he is domestic and usually affable. At a political convention where he knows he will be able to associate with men of like mind and interests, he is almost gregarious. Whether leading a parade, volunteering as a fire-fighter, or calling the town to witness an aurora borealis, he is a natural leader who takes the responsibilities of his position for granted and enjoys them. The fact is that hardly a week passed from one year's end to the other when relatives, personal or political friends, singly or in numbers, were not welcome as overnight or dinner guests. The squire was scrupulous in returning social obligations, and his Commencement receptions, a recognized feature of the most important event of the year, were annual affairs. To keep such a household going with leisurely grace requires a stable domestic routine and the desire on the part of a wife to be a helpmeet. There is every reason to believe that Edward Dickinson's wife found quite as much happiness in the life they thus created as he, who indeed was ever ready to count his blessings.

Some ten years elapsed, from the time Emily wrote the letters to Austin quoted above, before she found occasion to identify herself, and her relation to her family, to an outsider. Writing Higginson in 1862, she sketches, not a different father, but an isolated daughter: "I have a Brother and Sister – My Mother does not care for thought – and Father, too busy with his Briefs – to notice what we do – He buys me many Books – but begs me not to read them – because he fears they joggle the mind." In her initial conversation with Higginson eight years later, in 1870, she volunteered these remarks: "My father only reads on Sunday. He reads *lonely* and *rigorous* books. . . I never knew how to tell time by the clock till I was fifteen. My father thought he had taught me, but I did not understand and I was afraid to say I did not and afraid to ask anyone else lest he should know."

Colonel Higginson met Edward Dickinson very briefly at that time. He described her father as "thin, dry and speechless," adding "I saw what her life has been." It is most unlikely that Higginson did in fact see much. Edward Dickinson of course knew who Higginson was, for Higginson had been for some years an active participant in liberal causes many of which to Dickinson seemed visionary if not dangerous. Higginson was now a professional man of letters and with such men, as a class, Dickinson had little in common. He could be expansive enough when he chose. On this occasion he chose evidently to be dry and speechless.

In the same year Emily drew a one-sentence sketch for her young cousins, Louise and Frances Norcross, who had been intimate members of the Dickinson household since their childhood: "Father steps like Cromwell when he gets the kindlings." A letter to them in 1871 probes more deeply: "Father was very sick. I presumed he would die, and the sight of his lonesome face all day was harder than personal trouble. He is growing better, though physically reluctantly. I hope I am mistaken, but I think his physical life don't want to live any longer. You know he never played, and the straightest engine has its leaning hour."

Edward Dickinson was stricken in Boston on 16 June 1874, while delivering an address before the Massachusetts legislature favoring the proposed Hoosac Tunnel, later built to give rail connection between the northwestern part of the state and the east. The heart condition that probably had been depressing his spirits for some time proved fatal two hours after he had managed to get himself back to his hotel. Emily wrote her cousins:

We were eating our supper the fifteenth [sixteenth] of June, and Austin came in. He had a despatch in his hand, and I saw by his face we were all lost, though I didn't know how. He said that father was very sick, and he and Vinnie must go. The train had already gone. While horses were dressing, news came that he was dead. Father does not live with us now—he lives in a new house. Though it was built in an hour it is better than this. He hasn't any garden because he moved after gardens were made, so we take him the best flowers, and if we only knew he knew, perhaps we could stop crying.

Thrice during the next several months she set down reminiscences in letters to Higginson:

The last Afternoon that my Father lived, though with no premonition—I preferred to be with him, and invented an absence for Mother, Vinnie being asleep. He seemed peculiarly pleased as I oftenest stayed with myself, and remarked as the Afternoon withdrew, he "would like it not to end." His pleasure almost embarrassed me and my Brother coming—I suggested they walk. Next morning I woke him for the train—and saw him no more. His Heart was pure and terrible and I think no other like it exists. I am glad there is Immortality—but would have tested it myself—before intrusting him.

Home is so far from Home, since my Father died.

At the same time she expressed herself thus to her friend Mrs. Holland: "When I think of his firm Light—quenched so causelessly, it fritters the worth of much that shines. . . 'I say unto you,' Father would read at Prayers, with a militant Accent that would startle one . . . Thank you for the Affection. It helps me up the Stairs at Night, where as I passed my Father's Door—I used to think was safety." Eighteen months after his death she wrote to ask Colonel Higginson to accept Frothingham's *Theodore Parker* and George Eliot's *Poems*. "The last Books that my Father brought me I have felt unwilling to open, and had reserved them for you, because he had twice seen you."

There still survives a half-sheet of stationery, belonging to this period, headed "Dear Father – "and signed below "Emily." The space between is blank. It graphically illuminates her acute awareness that death severs the means of communication. One of her later reminiscences she sent to Mrs. Bowles in 1880. Samuel Bowles of the *Springfield Republican*, who died two years before, had been one of the closest friends of the family. "The last April that father lived, lived I mean below, there were several snow-storms, and the birds were so frightened and cold they sat by the kitchen door. Father went to the barn in his slippers and came back with a breakfast of grain for each, and hid himself while he scattered it, lest it embarrass them. Ignorant of the name or fate of their benefactor, their descendants are singing this afternoon."

The home in which Emily was born she elected to make in a physical sense exclusively her life. She was therefore at times intolerably lonely, and gained a sense of freedom by unburdening herself to outsiders like Higginson who would be understanding but not inquisitive in their responses. Saying to such a person that one's father read lonely and rigorous books, or that one's mother did not care for thought, was intended to stir sympathy for one's isolation. What she said was true, but it was not the whole truth, as she herself well knew.

It is to the credit of all members of the Dickinson family that each gave to the others a sense of personal identity. Each took for granted the right of all to run their own lives as they chose. Since such a point of view does not complain, it does not explain. It merely makes the necessary repairs after minor collisions.

One suspects there was a recognizable twinkle in the squire's eye when he presented his daughter with books which he begged her not to joggle her mind by reading. It is true that his own taste ran to such books in his library as Paley's *Principles*, Daniel Webster's *Works*, and Seth Williston's *Millennial Discourses*. Yet the children knew that the homestead was always ready to welcome

Samuel Bowles, whose gaiety and flashing wit could wholly re-claim a month of serious-mindedness. If soberer virtues often domi-nated, one adjusted to them as part of the price exacted of Dickin-sons, who had a status to maintain. The legal structure of Calvin-ism, with its provision for an elect, was congenial to Squire Dickin-son the lawyer and politician. So too was a spanking ride behind fast horses. Emily Norcross Dickinson, as wife, basked in the re-flected glow of her husband's good name. Thus he created an adult world where the love of all members of the family for each other could be like his for them, deep and lasting — but without demon-stration. In such a world the differences of opinion in matters of individual preference are essentially trivial. This truth Emily Dick-inson perceived and lived by from her youth, but she did not will-ingly accept it until after her father had died. Can there be an association between her feeling about her father and this poem which she sent to Colonel Higginson in January, 1876? The legal phraseology may so suggest, as well as the theme itself, which de-fines a constancy faithful merely unto death as abhorrent.

> "Faithful to the end" Amended
> From the Heavenly Clause —
> Constancy with a Proviso
> Constancy abhors —
>
> "Crowns of Life" are servile Prizes
> To the stately Heart,
> Given for the Giving, solely,
> No Emolument.

In the letters that Emily wrote to Austin in the early fifties, quoted earlier, it is their father who always stands in the forefront. One is conscious there is a mother, because she is seen coming to the door to welcome a sister or speed her son, after a vacation period, wiping a tear with the corner of her apron. But otherwise she is in the shadow, partially obscured by others or by the afterthought of Emily herself, who at the last minute remembers she had forgotten to mention her mother. The longest passage says this: "Mother never was busier than while we were away – what with fruit and plants and chickens and sympathizing friends she really was so hurried she hardly knew what to do." Thrice Emily singled out her mother for identification in writing or talking to Colonel Higginson, and in a manner that unmistakably identifies the mother-daughter relationship:

> My Mother does not care for thought.
> I never had a mother. I suppose a mother is one to whom you hurry when you are troubled.
> I always ran Home to Awe when a child, if anything befell me. He was an awful Mother, but I liked him better than none.

To Mrs. Holland she wrote in 1873: "I was thinking of thanking you for the kindness to Vinnie. She has no Father and Mother but me and I have no Parents but her."

Just a year after Edward Dickinson died, Mrs. Dickinson suffered a paralytic stroke. In 1878 she broke her hip, and though she never left her bed thereafter, she lingered until November 1882. The care of the helpless invalid Emily largely assumed. After her mother died she wrote Mrs. Holland: "We were never intimate Mother and Children while she was our Mother – but Mines in the same Ground meet by tunneling and when she became our Child, the Affection came." She spoke in the same tone to her Norcross cousins: "She was scarcely the aunt you knew. The great mission of pain had been ratified – cultivated to tenderness by persistent sorrow, so that a larger mother died than had she died before." The experience had wrought a new dimension in the lives of both.

Lavinia Norcross Dickinson was two years younger than her sister Emily. Since she too never married, and lived throughout her life in the house where both had been born, the lives of the sisters were closely knit. Both attended Amherst Academy, and it was on both that young college undergraduates called in the early fifties. A daguerreotype of Vinnie taken at that time confirms the tradition that she was pretty. Her face is oval, the features regular, the unblemished skin white. Her abundant dark hair remained lustrous and never altered its color. The sisters were devoted, each feeling a protectiveness about the other. Vinnie aggressively stood between Emily and the world in later years when Emily no longer could face contacts as far abroad as the living-room or the front door. Emily reciprocated with daily allegiances that can be traced in her correspondence. Vinnie's wit was pungent and her exuberant spirits made high adventure out of the commonplace. Since she enjoyed visiting and travel, and was a welcome guest in the homes of her friends, the vivid, salty accounts she brought back charmed Emily, who thus vicariously experienced the thrill of going a journey.

Like her mother, and unlike her sister, Lavinia was willing to undertake responsibility for routine domestic affairs. Emily wrote to her from Cambridge, whither she had gone in 1864 to stay with the Norcross cousins while undergoing treatment in Boston for a troublesome eye condition: "Love for All and dont work too hard, picking up after Chimneys – The Grass will cover it all up, and I can sweep, next Fall." The Hollands were fond of Vinnie, and looked forward to her occasional visits. They would share Emily's amusement at Vinnie's irrepressible energy: "Vinnie is far more hurried than Presidential Candidates – I trust in more distinguished ways, for *they* have only the care of the Union, but Vinnie the Universe –" On one subject only did the sisters seriously differ. Birds were to Emily more than a part of the landscape. They somehow symbolized the renewing creativeness of nature. She also for a period of years had been warmly attached to the large dog Carlo, a gift from her father. The companionship of the animal had been such that after 1866, when it died presumably full of years and canine wisdom, Emily never cared to have another. Vinnie liked cats, and kept not just one or two but on occasion several. To Emily who instinctively loved birds and dogs, a houseful of cats was a fell experience. She confided to Mrs. Holland in 1881: "Vinnie had four Pussies for Christmas Gifts – and two from her Maker, previous, making six, in toto, and finding Assassins for them, is my stealthy Aim." In the mid-sixties she had expressed her feelings in a poem.

His Bill is clasped – his Eye forsook –
His Feathers wilted low –
The Claws that clung, like lifeless Gloves
Indifferent hanging now –
The Joy that in his happy Throat
Was waiting to be poured
Gored through and through with Death, to be
Assassin of a Bird
Resembles to my outraged mind
The firing in Heaven,
On Angels – squandering for you
Their Miracles of Tune –

But it was Lavinia Dickinson who, after her sister's death, with single-minded devotion and against considerable odds, engineered the publication of Emily's poems. It is typical of the Dickinson respect for privacy that Lavinia was genuinely astonished, on going through her deceased sister's effects, when she made discovery of the poems, neatly arranged in the cherry bureau. Vinnie of course knew, as did everyone else, that Emily "wrote poetry," but no one, not even she, was even faintly aware of the degree to which Emily had identified herself with the very muse.

No one in the family understood Emily better than her brother William Austin Dickinson. It was he and he alone among the members who clearly saw through her stratagems of living, and recognized in her self-dramatization a device she adopted to stage her appearances before friends and the world in general. Austin was the eldest of the three children, and a year and a half older than Emily. An only son, intelligent, personable, sensitive, and outgoing, he was the apple of his father's eye. To Emily, as they were growing up, he was everything that a brother should be, and though the shining quality of their early intimacy was later lost, their mutual affection never abated.

Austin was graduated from Amherst College in 1850, and after a year of teaching at the Endicott School in Boston he attended Harvard Law School, receiving his degree in 1854. He returned to

Amherst where he remained in the practice of law until his death in 1895. On the resignation of his father in 1873 as treasurer of the College, he was appointed his father's successor. Like his father, he identified himself with church and community enterprises. He came to be everything that is implied in the phrase "solid citizen."

Emily's admiration for the character of her father was extended to include her brother, and her really voluminous correspondence with him during the years 1850–1854 is singularly warmhearted. Austin shared her taste in books and her love of beauty in nature. Yet as the years advanced, the differences between father and son became more marked. An instinctive warmheartedness left Austin without relish for the rough and tumble of politics, and his civic leadership did not extend beyond the perimeter of the village. He lived for and within the college and the town, overseeing the erection of new buildings as his father had done, but adding to the natural beauty of the place by well-planned landscaping. Did he busy himself with the minutiae of community improvements to sublimate a sense of frustration? Though Emily was the recluse and Austin the person of affairs, one senses that she knew that her accomplishments were substantial, but that his never quite matched his capabilities. The realization seems to have been clear to both. "Austin's Family went to Geneva," Emily wrote Mrs. Holland in 1875, "and Austin lived with us four weeks. It seemed peculiar – pathetic – and Antediluvian. We missed him while he was with us and missed him when he was gone." The sympathetic attachment of twenty years before was now irreparably destroyed, though the bonds of kinship would never be loosened.

While Austin was in law school he became engaged to Susan Huntington Gilbert. Vivacious, witty, and attractive, Sue was at the time one of Emily's dearest friends. Born in the same year, the girls had known each other casually from Amherst Academy days, and their friendship had become intimate by 1850. Sue's father, who kept a tavern in Deerfield, leased the Mansion House in Amherst in 1832, and moved thither with his wife and family of seven children. Orphaned when she was eleven, Sue, the youngest, was

Emily, Austin, and Lavinia Dickinson

Edward Dickinson

Emily Norcross Dickinson

Emily Dickinson about seventeen

reared in turn by an aunt in Geneva, New York, and an elder married sister residing in Amherst. She was thus in and out of Amherst during the forties. Her eldest brother Dwight meanwhile established himself successfully in Grand Haven, Michigan, and before Sue's marriage he took pleasure in assisting her financially. Her precarious security derived from such attention as others gave her, rather than from the stability of a home. Having to fend for herself gave her a knowledge of people and places which to Emily seemed the mark of a cosmopolitan person. And indeed by her nature Sue was different. Her mind and manners were well cultivated. She had an apt imagination and a talent for oral narrative and ready repartee that, after her marriage, came to make her gatherings social events. Her embellishments for the sake of the tale subordinated accuracy to color and, because they did not spare feelings, became in time embarrassing to her husband and Emily, and infuriated Vinnie.

She was, nevertheless, a stimulating companion, and no friend of Emily's youth absorbed her more than Sue, the one member of the family who came to know most about Emily's poetry. The two saw things in the same way, and felt the immediacy of books, of poetry especially. Sue's opulent nature and scintillating manner won Austin's heart, for his intense and warmhearted nature craved less austerity than that which his father found congenial. They were engaged on Thanksgiving Day 1853. In October of the following year Austin, his degree in law secured, planned to take Sue to Chicago. They had been thinking they might settle and grow up with the West. His instincts were right, for his fulfillment needed the stimulus of new ways to approach and do things, and especially of being out from under the unintentional domination of his father. Sue would visit her brother and they both would look Chicago over and measure their prospects. The moment proved to be the turning point in his life, and his decision not to go, but to remain in Amherst and enter his father's law office, indicates the persuasive nature of his father's character, as well perhaps as of Sue's. For Edward Dickinson offered to give him the land adjoining the homestead and to build a house on it for a wedding present. This he did, and on July 1, 1856, Austin and Susan were married, and shortly thereafter moved into their new home. The setting in which Emily Dickinson would act out the rest of her life was now staged.

Always possessive about her friendships, during her twenties Emily was inclined to be sentimental about them. For some dozen years, from 1848 until 1861, she adopted the signature "Emilie." It was part of the "little girl" cult that she was then affecting. In 1850 Donald Grant Mitchell's *Reveries of a Bachelor*, published over the pseudonym "Ik Marvel," had a very wide appeal for teenagers. Both Emily and Sue came under its romantic spell. The twenty-six-year-old bachelor muses sentimentally on friendship, love, and marriage, accompanied in his daydreams by his dog Carlo. Subtitled "A Book of the Heart," it transports the reader into regions of airy infinitudes. The girls thought its fancies and its language beyond criticism, and avidly awaited publication in the year following of its successor, *Dream Life*. Their abandonment to the empty phantasms of the first book had so depleted their emotions and clarified their judgments that the second they found quite unsatisfying.

The "ie" for "y" spelling of her name coincides with the years when Emily was vaguely yearning for some identity that would set her apart, and for some friend on whom she could rely for advice and stimulus in matters touching upon her poetry. She had probably written very few poems before Sue and Austin were married, but she had written some and she certainly had high hopes that the writing of poetry might be for her more than a pastime. Her attachment to Sue was closer at this time than to any other friend because Sue probably encouraged her more than others and perhaps seemed to Emily to have keener sensibilities. She had commented in 1851 in a letter to Sue that the two of them "please ourselves with the fancy that we are the only poets, and everyone else is *prose*." In 1858 the pleasure she took in the fact that Sue had become part of the family and was now a sister, she made the subject of a poem that she sent her, signed "Emilie," the first four stanzas of which give a summary of their past and present relationship.

One Sister have I in our house,
And one, a hedge away.
There's only one recorded,
But both belong to me.

One came the road that I came –
And wore my last year's gown –
The other, as a bird her nest,
Builded our hearts among.

She did not sing as we did –
It was a different tune –
Herself to her a music
As Bumble bee of June.

Today is far from Childhood –
But up and down the hills
I held her hand the tighter –
Which shortened all the miles –

A pet name for Sue was "Dolly," and thrice Emily incorporated it in poems. Two are composed in the affectionate mood of the lines above, but the very closeness of the women was bound to set up new stresses. One poem written in 1860, beginning "You love me – you are sure," concludes:

Be sure you're sure – you know –
I'll bear it better now . . .
Than when – a little dull Balm grown . . .
You sting – again!

In 1861 occurred the letter-exchange concerning the poem "Safe in their Alabaster Chambers," a version of which Emily had sent to Sue for criticism. Sue did not approve the second stanza. Emily therefore wrote a new stanza, and sent it across the hedge with the notation: "Perhaps this verse would please you better – Sue." Sue returned it, indicating that she liked it even less than the one she had disapproved. "It is remarkable as the chain lightening that blinds us hot nights in the Southern sky but it does not go with the ghostly shimmer of the first verse as well as the other one." The criticism led Emily to a third attempt, which she sent over in a note that makes clear that she felt Sue had missed the mark. She herself must have realized the inferiority of the third trial, for she never incorporated it in the poem. It is most unlikely that she ever again asked advice from Sue about her poetry. The note says: "Your praise is good – to me – because I *know* it *knows* – and *suppose* it *means*. Could I make you and Austin – proud – sometime – a great way off – 'twould give me taller feet." The second sentence tells much. By 1861 she was conscious of her destiny as a poet, even to point of confiding to Sue that she hopes someday to win honor and a name.

Over the years Emily continued to send copies of poems to Sue; in fact, she gave Sue nearly three hundred – a far larger number than went to anyone else. The impulses that prompted her to do so were several. Among them was a desire to share, to win regard from one whom she loved. In 1862 she wrote a very enigmatic poem. One cannot say surely that the person therein designated is in fact Sue, yet the nature of their relationship at this time strongly suggests the probability, the more so because their relationship is the sole one that gives the poem a meaning.

> Ourselves were wed one summer – dear –
> Your Vision – was in June –
> And when Your little Lifetime failed,
> I wearied – too – of mine –
>
> And overtaken in the Dark –
> Where You had put me down –
> By Some one carrying a Light –
> I – too – received the Sign.
>
> 'Tis true – Our Futures different lay –
> Your Cottage – faced the sun –
> While Oceans – and the North must be –
> On every side of mine

'Tis true, Your Garden led the Bloom,
For mine – in Frosts – was sown –
And yet, one Summer, we were Queens –
But You – were crowned in June –

You and I were once in close accord, she is saying. I always thought
that the way you saw things was the best possible way to see them,
and when anything troubled you, I was so close to you that I felt
it too. Deserted by you, someone else brought me the light which
has given me the right to the happiness which you had claimed.
I realize that our lives had to be lived differently. Certainty and
warmth lay ahead for you; uncertainty and isolation are my lot.
Although these differences must be acknowledged, we did once
share the same feeling that "we are the only poets, and everyone
else is *prose.*" But your fate was always to be in the sun.

There is no question that there were difficulties for Emily in
the early years of Sue's marriage, when Emily felt "dropped." Her
possessiveness may not always have been easy to cope with. Austin
and Sue's first child Ned, named for his grandfather Dickinson,
was born in 1861, and their daughter Martha five years later. As
Sue increasingly found new and varied interest outside, Emily was
progressively restricting her own, at least to outward appearance.
During the sixties and into the seventies the relationship of the
sisters stabilized into fairly frictionless grooves, but in the final
decade of Emily's life there are unmistakable indications that fric-
tions increased. To Emily, Sue's thoughts were expressed with more
glitter than illumination. "Austin said he should write you," she
told Mrs. Holland in 1877, "and that Sue w'd too – but he is over-
charged with care, and Sue with scintillation, and I fear they have
not." Early in 1881 in a letter to Higginson she seems clearly to
hint at some kind of alienation by referring to Sue as her "pseudo-
sister." And it is about this time that she sent Sue the note saying:
"With the exception of Shakespeare, you have told me of more
knowledge than any one living. To say that sincerely is strange
praise." The praise is indeed strange. One can only speculate what
Sue had taught her about the human heart.

The fact that the number of notes exchanged each year after 1877 increases might imply that Sue and Emily saw each other less often. The attachment was strained but both seem to have been resolved that it should never be broken, and one senses that on Emily's side there is the haunting wish to be a sister to the Sue who might have been. And then an event occurred that shattered all preconceptions. It altered indeed the lives of all the Dickinsons.

Death of friends, to which Emily had always been peculiarly sensitive, became more frequent after she passed her fiftieth year. But the blow that prostrated her and drained her nervous energy to a point beyond which she could never fully regain her strength was the death of her eight-year-old nephew Gilbert. Thomas Gilbert Dickinson was a late arrival in the household of Austin and Susan. Ned and Mattie were very nearly grown up; Ned was past twenty and Mattie nearly seventeen. Both were dear to their Aunt Emily, but they had never found the special place in her heart that she reserved for their much younger brother. Indeed, Gilbert's arrival had seemed heaven-sent to the members of both households. It had helped relieve the petty but mounting tensions between Sue and Vinnie which always took their toll on Emily. Most important it had brought Austin and Sue new perspectives and new concord. In Gilbert, Austin could look hopefully forward to a continuation of his branch of the Dickinson family. Ned had never been robust, his periods of illness were increasing, and he could perform the routines of living only by a careful economy of his strength. He was a gentle, fine-textured person, but not fated to survive his thirty-seventh year.

But Gilbert was different. Handsome, healthy, vivacious, and outgoing, he was loved as much by the grandmother and aunts at the homestead as he was by his adoring brother and sister, and he was at home equally in either house. He and his playmates were allowed to tramp at will through Aunt Emily's kitchen. His better remarks became family bywords. Then without warning, and with a suddenness for which no one was prepared, it happened. Gilbert was stricken with typhoid fever early in October 1883. On the fifth of the month he died.

For Emily Dickinson, who thought she had plumbed every emotional depth death could offer, this latest stroke was overwhelming. Must one be required by well-intentioned platitude to hear that the worst is not so long as we can say "This is the worst?" Involved in Gilbert's death, as she well knew, was the stable happiness of all the members of her family as well as her own.

The most moving letter that Emily Dickinson wrote in all her many years of correspondence she addressed now to Sue. That is to say, the form it takes is that of a letter, but in a truer sense it is a poem, an elegy of surpassing eloquence addressed to the memory of Gilbert. One never tires of reading it, and reading it again. Here there is no cry of anguish, no flinching, no panic in the face of chaos, no suggestion of laceration. She did not write the letter until she had mastered her nerve and glimpsed in vision the unfathomable harmonies which now became her memories of the little playmate. A sense of vibrancy, rapid motion, and light predominate, and the figures of speech tumble over each other: the boy is a passenger panting, prattling, whirling like a dervish, soaring; she sees him in the star, and meets his velocity in all flying things; he is light, and dawn, and meridian, and the swift-footed Ajax.

Dear Sue –

The Vision of Immortal Life has been fulfilled –
How simply at the last the Fathom comes! The Passenger and not the Sea, we find surprises us –
Gilbert rejoiced in Secrets –
His Life, was panting with them – With what menace of Light he cried "Don't tell, Aunt Emily"! Now my ascended Playmate must instruct *me*. Show us, prattling Preceptor, but the way to thee!
He knew no niggard moment – His Life was full of Boon – The Playthings of the Dervish were not so wild as his –
No crescent was this Creature – He traveled from the Full –
Such soar, but never set –
I see him in the Star, and meet his sweet velocity in everything that

43

flies – His Life was like the Bugle, which winds itself away, his Elegy an echo – his Requiem ecstasy –

Dawn and Meridian in one.

Wherefore would we wait, wronged only of Night, which he left for us –

Without a speculation, our little Ajax spans the whole –

Pass to thy Rendezvous of Light,
Pangless except for us –
Who slowly ford the Mystery
Which thou hast leaped across!

Emily.

The letter does more than sublimate her grief. It gives wholeness of spirit back to Sue.

III

FRIENDS: Ecstatic Instants

IT WAS THE SECOND OF THE THREE WORLDS in which Emily Dickinson lived, the world of friends, that she termed her "estate." It was the one too in which she felt her greatest insecurity, for she associated it with fear of loss. One may be deprived of friends by indifference or estrangement or — most incessantly — by death. "Perhaps Death – gave me awe for friends – striking sharp and early," she wrote Colonel Higginson when she was thirty-two, "for I held them since – in a brittle love – of more alarm, than peace." It is also the world in which she lived with an absorbed intensity. "Dear Mr. Bowles," she had written in 1858, embracing the whole family, "I hope your cups are full. I hope your vintage is untouched. In such a porcelain life one likes to be *sure* that all is well lest one stumble upon one's hopes in a pile of broken crockery. My friends are my 'estate.' Forgive me then the avarice to hoard them!"

The intensity of her emotion about friendship gradually deepened to such an extent that she avoided direct contacts, or fled to escape them. At first only the casual associations were affected, but in time those with people whom she knew well. In 1859 she told Mrs. Holland that she had been spending the evening with a friend when "someone rang the bell and I ran, as is my custom." She was wryly amused that the compulsion should be, but she was powerless either to explain or govern it. "Sunset at night – is natural," she wrote; eclipses are predictable and can be scientifically explained:

> But do one face us suddenly –
> Jehovah's Watch – is wrong.

She gave her witness even before 1860 to the toll exacted of one thus sensitively wrought.

> For each extatic instant
> We must an anguish pay
> In keen and quivering ratio
> To the extasy.

The exuberance of living overwhelmed her. Each new excitement became a heady liquor that made her stagger. "I can wade Grief," she exclaims in 1861, "But the least push of Joy/ Breaks up my feet – / And I tip – drunken." On one occasion her distress must have been acute, because it involved Samuel Bowles, one of her own and her family's closest friends.

Samuel Bowles of Springfield, but three years older than Austin, was on his way to becoming, at the age of thirty-five, one of the best-known journalists in the country. Liberal and independent in his thinking, by 1878, the year of his early death, he had made himself a leader of American opinion on political as well as social issues. In the 1840's he took over his father's *Springfield Daily Republican,* and by 1860 had made it national in scope. His editorials were written with a clarity and pithiness that gave stature to his journal and made its name a household word throughout New England and beyond.

Though Bowles might be irritably tense at his desk, in his home or with friends he was relaxed and expansive. His travels in this country and abroad were extensive and frequent, and he knew intimately many of the great of his day. No man was more welcome as a guest or companion than he, for his engaging personality revealed itself with singular charm. Tall, slightly stooped, with aquiline nose and piercing eyes, he had from her youth won special affection from Emily. His death from sheer exhaustion, coming so soon after the death of her father, was a blow that depleted her own energies. On learning from Sue in 1885 that Merriam's two-volume *Life* of Bowles was scheduled for publication, she sent Sue a note enclosing an elegy, "Though the great Waters sleep," and adding a thumbnail sketch that catches the spirit of his individuality with graphic penetration: "You remember his swift way of wringing and flinging away a Theme, and others picking it up and gazing bewildered after him, and the prance that crossed his Eye at such times was unrepeatable." In her last year she still felt the kinship of a quality in spirit that was somewhat like her own.

Bowles was abroad during the summer of 1862, and Emily wrote him twice. In the first letter she said: "I have the errand from my heart – I might forget to tell it. Would you please come home? The long life's years are scant, and fly away, the Bible says, like a told story – and sparing is a solemn thing, somehow, it seems to me – and I grope fast, with my fingers, for all are out of my sight I own, to get it nearer." The tone of eager anticipation in the second is still more insistent: "I tell you, Mr. Bowles, it is a suffering to have a sea – no care how blue – between your soul and you . . . I've learned to read the steamer place in newspapers now. It's 'most like shaking hands with you, or more like your ringing at the door." Most certainly she wished to see him.

But the fact is that when he had returned and made a call in Amherst late in November, she remained in her room and sent a note to Bowles, who was in the sitting-room below. "Dear Friend, – I cannot see you. You will not less believe me. That you return to us alive is better than a summer, and more to hear your voice below than news of any bird." Bowles was amused and evidently wrote to twit her, perhaps enclosing a miniature bat, telling her that even though she had forgotten him, he had remembered her. Her reply attempts an explanation, but since she herself did not understand the nature of her malady, one is touched by the pathetic character of the apology.

Dear friend. I did not need the little Bat – to enforce your memory – for that can stand alone, like the best Brocade – but it was much – that far and ill, you recollected me – Forgive me if I prize the Grace – superior to the Sign. Because I did not see you, Vinnie and Austin, upbraided me – They did not know I gave my part that they might have the more – but then the Prophet had no fame in his immediate Town –

My Heart led all the rest – I think that what we *know* – we can endure
that others doubt, until their faith be riper. And so, dear friend, who
knew me, I make no argument – to you –

Did I not want to see you? Do not the Phebes want to come? Oh
They of little faith! I said that I was glad that you were alive – Might
it bear repeating? Some phrases are too fine to fade – and Light but just
confirms them – Few absences could seem so wide as your's has done,
to us – If 'twas a larger face – or we a smaller Canvas – we need not
know – now you have come –

We hope often to see you – Our poverty – entitles us – and friends
are nations in themselves – to supersede the Earth. . .

Since Bowles was scarcely more than four years older than she,
he was actually of her own generation, yet she never referred to
him except as "Mr. Bowles," or "Mr. Sam." The salutation in her
letters to him is either "Dear Mr. Bowles" or "Dear friend." Mrs.
Bowles was "Mary" to her, but Emily was never really intimate with
Mary Bowles who, as the mother of ten children born during the
fifties and sixties, was seldom long absent from her household.
Bowles himself, though devoted to his wife and family, was a man
who craved and found intellectual stimulus in the company of
others, both men and women, or through correspondence with
them. By nature Emily gravitated toward those who were vibrant,
witty, perceptive. She was especially attracted by persons for whom
she felt an awe because their intricate natures, affinitive to hers,
made them seem unfathomable. As she later recalled about Bowles,
it was the prance across his eye that had fascinated her.

But the very nature of her relationship to him gave him privi-
leges he greatly enjoyed and that he alone would dare to take. The
story has been told that once he called upstairs to her: "Emily, you
wretch! No more of this nonsense! I've traveled all the way from
Springfield to see you. Come down at once." She is said to have
complied and never to have been more brilliant. There is every
reason to believe the story is true, except that instead of calling her
a "wretch," he said: "You damned rascal!" The letter she wrote to
him after a call he made during 1877 concludes: "It is strange that

the most intangible thing is the most adhesive." She signed the letter "Your 'Rascal,'" adding: "I washed the Adjective."

The anticipation of friends was so great an excitement that actually to talk to them required more nervous energy than she felt she could muster. Her relationship with friends was for her an occult experience. "Nature assigns the Sun," she wrote Mrs. Holland:

> That – is Astronomy –
> Nature cannot enact a Friend –
> That – is Astrology.

Friends being her "estate," she feels

> 'Tis little I – could care for Pearls –
> Who own the ample sea –

Twice she explained her predicament to Colonel Higginson, phrasing her thought as aphorisms, as truths applicable to all human nature: "To seek enchantment, one must always flee." "Emblem is immeasurable – that is why it is better than Fulfillment, which can be drained." She describes in a poem written in 1862 exactly how the intensity of anticipation gave way to panic at the moment of fulfillment.

> I think the longest Hour of all
> Is when the Cars have come –
> And we are waiting for the Coach –
> It seems as though the Time
>
> Indignant – that the Joy was come –
> Did block the Gilded Hands –
> And would not let the Seconds by –
> But slowest instant – ends –
>
> The Pendulum begins to count –
> Like little Scholars – loud –
> The steps grow thicker – in the Hall –
> The Heart begins to crowd –

> Then I – my timid service done –
> Tho' service 'twas, of Love –
> Take up my little Violin –
> And further North – remove.

Of course in a truer sense she was not retreating from life, but living it with an exuberance few people experience so incessantly. "Every day," she wrote her Norcross cousins, "life feels mightier, and what we have the power to be, more stupendous. . . I know I love my friends – I feel it far in here where neither blue nor black eye goes, and fingers cannot reach."

> Elysium is as far as to
> The very nearest Room,
> If in that Room a Friend await
> Felicity or Doom –
>
> What fortitude the Soul contains,
> That it can so endure
> The accent of a coming Foot –
> The opening of a Door –

The forces that possessed her, when thus controlled, give incandescence to language expressing casual experience.

"Are Friends Delight or Pain?" she asks herself. "To live is so startling," she told Higginson, "it leaves but little room for other occupations though Friends are if possible an event more fair."

> Wonder – is not precisely Knowing
> And not precisely Knowing not –
> A beautiful but bleak condition
> He has not lived who has not felt –
>
> Suspense – is. his maturer Sister –
> Whether Adult Delight is Pain
> Or of itself a new misgiving –
> This is the Gnat that mangles men –

Colonel Higginson paid his first visit to Emily Dickinson in 1870, and in a letter to his wife written in the evening of the same

August day he gives the fullest statement any direct observer has recorded of her attitude toward the way of life she had chosen. The impressions are both in her own words as he recalled them, and in his.

"I find ecstasy in living – the mere sense of living is joy enough." I asked if she never felt want of employment, never going off the place, and never seeing any visitor. "I never thought of conceiving that I could ever have the slightest approach to such a want in all future time" (and added) "I feel that I have not expressed myself strongly enough."

He then went on: "I never was with any one who drained my nerve power so much. Without touching her, she drew from me. I am glad not to live near her."

The quality that Higginson perceived is precisely that which all who knew her felt. By 1870, though much of her poetry was written, Emily Dickinson was still a person whose intensity was so striking that strangers might well say they were glad not to live near her. No one was more aware of the draining effect in personal contacts than she herself. Her poems expressing the need to be abstemious of friends, such acts as withholding herself from so cherished a friend as Bowles, are thoughts and acts dictated by the forces that possessed her.

> Who never wanted – maddest Joy
> Remains to him unknown –
> The Banquet of Abstemiousness
> Defaces that of Wine –

Though one is tempted to find in the total retreat of her later years an element of the neurotic, the fact seems clear that she was possessed to a most uncommon degree by emotional responses so acute as to be painful to herself and others. One thus understands why letters increasingly became her chosen medium of communication. She wrote Colonel Higginson in 1869: "A Letter always feels to me like immortality because it is the mind alone without corporeal friend. Indebted in our talk to attitude and accent – there seems a spectral power in thought that walks alone." "A Letter is a joy of Earth," she wrote in the last year of her life. "It is denied the Gods." The two versions of "Going to Him! Happy letter!" and "Going to Her! Happy Letter!" are a paean to letter-writing, and together they embrace all friendships. The transport felt on receiving letters she memorializes in "The Way I read a Letter's this," where she locks her door to insure privacy, then peruses the letter to discover how infinite she is to someone:

> To no one that You – know –
> And sigh for lack of Heaven – but not
> The Heaven God bestow –

In later years almost all poems were intended for enclosure in letters to friends. It was the receiving and sending of letters that now constituted her "estate," and on them she lavished as much care as she had earlier devoted to her poems, writing them in first draft, correcting, polishing, then dispatching the finished copy. In some instances her pleasure in the choice of a phrase was such that she incorporated identical paragraphs in letters to different correspondents.

Letters gave her the means of selecting her society, and thus spared her from encounters of the sort implied in her query to Higginson: "How do most people live without any thoughts"? They also spared her the need to explain her remarks: "All men say 'What' to me," she told the Colonel.

> Experiment to me
> Is every one I meet
> If it contain a Kernel?

Her conclusion is that "Meat within, is requisite/ To Squirrels and to Me." Letters also allowed her to indulge her whimsy for incorporating lines of poetry as prose, thus leaving the recipient uncertain where prose leaves off and poetry begins. Such is often her method when she acknowledges a kindness by returning a flower accompanied by a verse, or when she sends a greeting. On the occasion that E. P. Crowell, professor of English at Amherst, and his wife left for a trip abroad in 1885, she sent Mrs. Crowell such a note.

> Is it too late to touch you, Dear?
> We this moment knew –
> Love Marine and Love terrene –
> Love celestial too –
>
> I give his Angels charge –

By the mid-seventies when her seclusion was nearly absolute, her refusal to see old friends was determined by the fact that the nervous drain during such encounters had become exhausting beyond her power to cope with them. The idea of an affection which in the presence of friends gives way to panic made her feel guilty. Even in the mid-sixties she sensed her dilemma, because she wrote Mrs. Holland: "Shame is so intrinsic in a strong affection we must all experience Adam's reticence." Her feeling of nakedness she more than once identifies with Eve's discovery: "In all the circumference of expression," she wrote late in life, "those guileless words of Adam and Eve never were surpassed. 'I was afraid and hid myself.'"

Only the worksheet draft of the following poem survives, but it tells an interesting story.

> I shall not murmur if at last
> The ones I loved below
> Permission have to understand
> For what I shunned them so –
> Divulging it would rest my Heart
> But it would ravage their's –
> Why, Katie, Treason has a Voice –
> But mine – dispels – in Tears.

It is a penciled note, signed "Emily," written on the first and third pages of a sheet of correspondence stationery. Though it has been folded as if for enclosure in an envelope, it obviously was never sent, for a small section of the fourth page has been used to set down further trial lines:

> We shun because we prize her Face
> Lest sight's ineffable disgrace
> Our Adoration stain

She has marginally suggested alternative readings for two words. For *sight's*, *proof's*, and for *stain*, both *mar* and *flaw*. Apparently dissatisfied with the finished poem, she turned the sheet over to make a fresh start and clarify the obscurity. The final result, presumably sent to Kate (Scott) Anthon,* can only be conjectured, but apparently she is trying to explain to Katie her inability to see her: "My not being able to see you is not because I don't care ('Treason') – but because I should be speechless. I prefer to keep my dream of you rather than see the reality which might mar that dream ('sight's ineffable disgrace')." The lines are in the handwriting of 1877, the year Mrs. Anthon revisited Amherst as a guest of her old school friend Susan Dickinson. In the late fifties and early sixties she had been Sue's guest on occasion, and had come to know Emily. The acquaintanceship appears to have lapsed after Katie's marriage to John Anthon in 1866. So many years have passed since they met that Emily's customary panic is more acute than usual. The poem "We shun it ere it comes" was similarly inspired. Professor J. K. Chickering had been very helpful at the time of Mrs. Dickinson's death in November 1882, and shortly thereafter he asked if he might call on Emily. She requested a postponement, planning to see him later, after his return from a trip, but when the time came she found herself, as the poem in the note she wrote tells him, panicked with "dismay."

Dear friend – I had hoped to see you, but have no grace to talk,

---

* There were only four other "Katies" whom Emily knew, but the lines would have been inappropriate if applied to any of them. Her aunt Katie Sweetser she always saw, and addressed as "Aunt Katie"; Kate Hitchcock, a childhood friend, passed out of her life early, as did Kate Newman. Kate Holland, the daughter of Dr. and Mrs. J. G. Holland, she did not know.

and my own Words so chill and burn me, that the temperature of other Minds is too new an Awe –

> We shun it ere it comes,
> Afraid of Joy,
> Then sue it to delay
> And lest it fly,
> Beguile it more and more –
> May not this be
> Old Suitor Heaven,
> Like our dismay at thee?

She signed the letter "Earnestly, E. Dickinson." Thus can one see the pattern of her escape from debilitating encounters, especially the casual meetings with friends from a past which no longer had a present. The pattern was adopted sometime in the early sixties, shortly after her thirtieth birthday, and she never departed from it. But the withdrawals even from the beginning can be associated with the stage fright of actors and the self-indulgence of prima donnas. Such is certainly apparent in her letter to Bowles after his call in November 1862. She dramatized herself by remaining upstairs to let Vinnie and Austin "have the more" of his time. Her life like her poetry was dramatic. Each day separately enacts itself, and she identified herself with each separate day of living. "Drama's Vitallest Expression," she wrote in 1863, "is the Common Day/ That arise and set about us." Hamlet to himself would have been Hamlet, she points out, had there been no Shakespeare.

> It were infinite enacted
> In the Human Heart –
> Only Theatre recorded
> Owner cannot shut –

Inevitably such an artist learns how to plan her exits and entrances.

In 1881 young David Peck Todd came to Amherst as director of the college observatory. Vinnie immediately urged that he call at the Dickinson homestead with his bride, Mabel Loomis Todd. Mrs. Todd was charming and an able musician who played Emily's piano as generously as both sisters could wish. Mrs. Todd recalled that Emily's responses were eager and her voice touched with a breathless surprise as she commented on selections which she probably had never heard so well rendered. But though Emily Dickinson wrote notes of appreciation to Mrs. Todd, and sent verses to her, the fact is that Mrs. Todd never once saw her face to face. Emily Dickinson always hovered out of sight and thereby played her part beyond the glare of the footlights.

"I'd rather recollect a setting," she wrote in the mid-seventies, "Than own a rising sun . . ."

> Because in going is a Drama
> Staying cannot confer.

Her stratagems, like her poetry, once thought to be eccentric, were part of the drama of her existence. She saw only those she chose to see. She conversed in aphorisms. She dressed immaculately and only in white. To small children she was always accessible, and to them she opened her heart and her cookie jar. She secured her privacy by the stalwart aid of her sister and their faithful Irish maid. She organized her daily routines so that she could live and think and express her thoughts as she herself wished them lived and expressed. Her life, like her art, was planned with utmost economy.

The turning point in Emily Dickinson's life came in her late twenties. It was then that she felt assurance of her originality and her potential as an artist, and it was then that she began to work out her testament of beauty under the creative impulse of her love for Charles Wadsworth. By 1862 she accepted the judgment that her verse was not for publication, and realized that thenceforth in her lifetime she must expect to share it with private audiences only. But the impulse to create was at flood, and she tolerated no interference from routine distractions.

> The Soul selects her own Society –
> Then – shuts the Door –
> To her divine Majority –
> Present no more –

The lines, written at the time, can be taken as a motto for her own guidance, since by now she had made most of her selections, and was shutting the door on the rest. Her emotions had altered. Whereas in her schooldays and early twenties her response to affective moods had been diffuse and sweeping, they now began to focus in a narrow, sharper beam. Prior to the change, passages in her letters were often phrased like this to Mrs. Holland, written in the mid-fifties: "My only sketch, profile, of Heaven is a large, blue sky, bluer and larger than the *biggest* I have seen in June, and in it are my friends – all of them – every one of them – those who are with me now, and those who were 'parted' as we walked, and 'snatched up to Heaven.'"

Her early attachments were possessive and sentimental. One of her closest girlhood friends, Abiah Root, came to Amherst Academy for a short time in 1844–1845. She and Emily corresponded during the next ten years, until Abiah married the Reverend Samuel W. Strong in 1854, and settled into a life of domestic piety. Emily's letters to her, though long, are dull, for Abiah's life – and probably her mind, though her own letters do not survive – followed conventional patterns, and Emily was not stirred to thought. Emily's last known letter sounds very much like a terminal one, concluding an intimacy that had come to have little meaning for either. "You asked me to come and see you – I must speak of that. I thank you Abiah, but I dont go from home, unless emergency leads me by the hand, and then I do it obstinately, and draw back if I can. Should I ever leave home, which is improbable, I will with much delight, accept your invitation; till then, my dear Abiah, my warmest thanks are your's, but dont expect me."

Another early friendship, with Jane Humphrey, was likewise important, but the key in which it was pitched is the same, and it ended when Jane married. A year older than Emily, Jane came to the Academy from Southwick and returned to the Academy to teach in 1848 after her graduation from Mount Holyoke. She accepted other teaching positions during the fifties, until she married William H. Wilkinson of Montgomery, Alabama, in 1858. Thus was severed the second of two early intimacies. The fact is that what had been or seemed to be parallel ways for Emily and her close friends before 1858 thereafter diverged. Since Sue had now become part of the family, Emily seemed to think that through her she could link the past with the future. But Emily was striking into a new territory where there was indeed little out of past intimacies that she found usable. Though she had been fond of her cousin John Graves, whom she saw occasionally in later years, and of his friend Henry Vaughan Emmons, she had no close friends among any of the young men she had known in her youth, with the possible exception of Benjamin Newton. Since that friendship bears directly upon her development as a poet, it is left for later discussion.

The meaningful associations in Emily Dickinson's life developed, for the most part, after 1858. Certain neighbors during the last decade or so, by deeper thoughtfulness, won her heart, like Mrs. Edward Tuckerman, Mrs. Henry Hills, and Mrs. Howard Sweetser. Two important friendships she initiated herself, those with Charles Wadsworth and with Thomas Wentworth Higginson. That with Helen Hunt Jackson was thrust upon her. Three others were initiated by her father's friendships. They were begun, and continued until death broke the ties, quite literally under his aegis: with the Bowleses, the Hollands, and with Otis Lord. The last came to have in the final five or six years of her life a transcendent importance to her as a person, though not as a poet, for by the time she fell in love with him her writing of verse was a habit and for the most part an improvisation.

It is true that Emily exchanged notes with Sue over the years, but the exchange after Sue's marriage is not strictly a correspondence. The letters that passed between Wadsworth and her — all but one — are destroyed, but they were of great importance to her. The correspondence with Judge Lord began late in life, and the few drafts that survive indicate how deeply in love with him she became. But passing over those relationships for the moment, one may say that at the level of sisterly devotion, no two friendships over the years were of greater importance to Emily than those with

Mrs. Holland and with the Norcross cousins. Both associations lasted throughout the remaining thirty years of her life, and never fluctuated in their warmth.

It was the young cousins Loo and Fanny Norcross who seem to have been able to stabilize Emily's need to adjust to such minor realities as she perforce had to live with: relatives who came and went, spring housecleaning, or Vinnie's cats. The girls also gave willing ear to Emily's penchant for gossip, wherein she indulged when she knew by experience that her confidences were kept inviolate. In other words, the cousins helped Emily bridge her world of absolutes and transitives.

The lineal and collateral branches of Dickinsons and Norcrosses seemed numberless. Many of them Emily never saw, and some she scarcely heard of. Her paternal grandparents had left Amherst when she was two years old and both were dead before she was ten. Her grandfather Norcross was married a second time, after the death of his first wife in 1829, to the woman about whom Emily had remarked to Abiah that she would as soon allude to anything so frivolous as a hippodrome in her presence as she would think of popping a firecracker in the hearing of Peter the Great. The Norcross grandparents survived until the Dickinson children were well grown, and were occasional visitors in the Amherst homestead. Emily had roomed with a cousin, Emily Norcross, at Mount Holyoke, but never alluded to her thereafter. One gathers that on the whole the Norcrosses were respectable but dull.

Of the many Dickinson aunts, uncles, and cousins, a few were affectionately esteemed over the years, but none was a shaping force in her life. Among members of the family, on either side, only two persons ever became intimate with Emily. They were the cousins Louise and Frances Norcross. Mrs. Dickinson had always been especially fond of her youngest sister, Lavinia, who married a cousin, Loring Norcross. Their two daughters, Loo and Fanny, respectively twelve and seventeen years younger than Emily, were orphaned when their parents died in the early sixties.

The friendships with Mrs. Holland and with the Norcross girls were of equal intimacy but answered different needs. One side of Emily's nature wished to remain unmatured, to think as a child and act as one. With the Norcrosses she never felt compelled to grow up. Spinsters all, the three could share attitudes in common about the world of other people's husbands and children. It was to them that Emily sent her last two-word note from her deathbed. With them she chatted freely, and she eagerly awaited their occasional visits to Amherst. She felt security in their boarding house in Cambridge when her eye condition made necessary extended sojourns near a Boston specialist in 1864 and 1865. Conventional, shy, and genteel, they never taxed their cousin with thought or bothered her with demands. They seem always to have stirred in Emily an elder sister's protective devotion, and continued through the years to be her "Little Cousins," or "Dear Ones." They on their part repaid the compliment by adopting some of her own idiosyncrasies of dress and behavior. Together they all played the game of "little-girlhood," and even in the eighties Emily could write them thus: "Mother heard Fanny telling Vinnie about her graham bread. She would like to taste it. Will Fanny please write Emily how, and not too inconvenient? Every particular, for Emily is dull, and she will pay in gratitude, which, though not canned like quinces, is fragrantest of all we know. Tell us just how and where they are, and if October sunshine is thoughtful of their heads." The mature side of Emily turned for sisterhood to Mrs. Holland.

The forebears of both the Hollands had been Valley people for several generations. As a boy, Josiah Gilbert Holland had determined to follow a professional career. He studied medicine and at twenty-five, after the prescribed two years of training, he began his practice in Springfield. Tall, erect, dignified, with straight black hair and black eyes, he won the attention of Elizabeth Chapin, four years his junior. The attraction was mutual, and the couple were married in 1845. It was a union of singular felicity. By temperament she was vivacious and witty, and in physique small or, as Emily later remarked "birdlike." Both the Hollands were outgoing in their friendships and loved for their graciousness. The Doctor soon came to realize that his avocation, writing poems and prose sketches, was in truth absorbing more of his time and interest than the practice of medicine, which he therefore decided to abandon. After a sojourn in the South, where he wrote a lively account of his travels that was published in installments in the *Springfield Daily Republican,* he returned to Springfield, and at Samuel Bowles's invitation he became in 1849 the associate editor of the newspaper. Thus by the time he was thirty he had established himself in his career. In 1851, so widespread was the favor won by his writing that Amherst College conferred on him an honorary Master of Arts degree. Certainly about this time, either directly from his Amherst associations or through the Bowleses, Dr. Holland became acquainted with the Dickinsons. In 1853 he took Mrs. Holland to call on them, and in September of that year both Emily and Lavinia returned the call by a visit to Springfield. Dr. Holland's reputation as author and lecturer had become national by the time he was forty, and in the ensuing years brought him substantial rewards. In 1867 he ended his connection with the *Republican.* After travel abroad with his wife and three children, he launched *Scribner's Monthly* in 1870, and soon moved to New York. He was able to attract excellent writers and, at the time of his death in 1881, the magazine was recognized as one of the leading literary journals.

Though Emily Dickinson had first known and always admired "the Doctor," as she called him, it was the independent-minded, candid, witty, sweet-tempered Mrs. Holland who became her "Little Sister." The quality of the intimacy, and the degree to which it was a part of her maturest nature, becomes immediately apparent in the letters that she wrote Mrs. Holland. Though she conveys her thought in aphorisms, she utters it without affectation. As in her poems, there is at times a haunting quality in her prose expressions, conferring a grace upon the commonplace. In October 1870, while the Germans were besieging Paris, she concluded a letter to Mrs. Holland thus:

Life is the finest secret. So long as that remains, we must all whisper. With that sublime exception I had no clandestineness. It was lovely to see you and I hope it may happen again. These beloved accidents must become more frequent. We are by September and yet my flowers are bold as June. Amherst has gone to Eden. To shut our eyes is Travel. The Seasons understand this. How lonesome to be an Article! I mean – to have no soul. An Apple fell in the night and a Wagon stopped. I suppose the Wagon ate the Apple and resumed it's way. How fine it is to talk. What Miracles the news is! Not Bismark but ourselves.

Or the mood could be narrative and witty. In April 1881 she wrote:

Did you know that Father's "Horace" had died – the "Cap'n Cuttle" of Amherst? He had lived with us always, though was not congenial – so his loss is a pang to Tradition, rather than Affection. I am sure you remember him. He is the one who spoke patronizingly of the Years, of Trees he sowed in "26," or Frosts he met in "20," and was so legendary that it seems like the death of the College Tower, our first Antiquity. I remember he was at one time disinclined to gather the Winter Vegetables till they had frozen, and when Father demurred, he replied "Squire, ef the Frost is the Lord's Will, I dont popose to stan in the way of it." I hope a nearer inspection of that "Will" has left him with as ardent a bias in it's favor.

Nothing she wrote is more graphic and at the same time more tender and lyrical than the description, late in 1883, of her shattered world after Gilbert's death.

Sweet Sister. Was that what I used to call you? I hardly recollect, all seems so different. I hesitate which word to take, as I can take but few and each must be in the chiefest, but recall that Earth's most graphic transaction is placed within a syllable, nay, even a gaze.

The Physician says I have "Nervous prostration." Possibly I have – I do not know the Names of Sickness. The Crisis of the sorrow of so many years is all that tires me. As Emily Bronte to her Maker, I write to my Lost "Every Existence would exist in thee." The tender consternation for you was much eased by the little Card, which spoke "better" as loud as a human Voice. Please, Sister, to wait. "Open the Door, open the Door, they are waiting for me," was Gilbert's sweet command in delirium. *Who* were waiting for him, all we possess we would give to know. Anguish at last opened it, and he ran to the little Grave at his Grandparents' feet. All this and more, though *is* there more? More than Love and Death? Then tell me it's name!

Such writing imparts durability to circumstances which begin as private, passing experience.

Ellen Glasgow's autobiography, *The Woman Within,* appeared in 1954. Published nine years after Miss Glasgow's death, it is the artful but uncontrived setting forth of recollections and judgments by one of the foremost American writers of the twentieth century. Ellen Glasgow was twelve years old when Emily Dickinson died, but even had they been contemporaries they would hardly have seemed to be sharers of the same world. Ellen Glasgow traveled extensively, and as hostess or guest, over the years, of many of the literary great on both sides of the Atlantic she was intimately a part of the current literary scene which she helped direct. She early secured her rank as artist and each successive book gave her added stature. Her themes were built on situations she created from her knowledge of the society in which she lived, and they always deal with people. Thus her achievement of rank in her own lifetime, her associations and her way of living, her approach to her art and her very themes would seem to offer no ready design by which the lives of the two writers might be compared. Yet there are striking parallels. Neither married and both were twice in love. Both were great artists whose lives presented smooth surfaces. Beneath the surface both felt personal frustrations which they stoically concealed. Ellen Glasgow in her autobiography speaks frankly of her unhappy love affairs, and comments that of one thing she is sure: that it is the law of woman's nature that the memory of longing survives the more fugitive memory of fulfillment. It was the destiny of Emily Dickinson that her memory of longing for the man with whom she first fell in love in her late twenties gave her a maturity that until then she had lacked. It enlarged and deepened her sympathies even as it drove her to a distraction that she seems to have feared she could not mentally survive. It stirred her talents into creative activity and in fact made her a poet. Her love for the Reverend Charles Wadsworth may well have been the single most important event in her life, and its force continued to give direction to her productive capabilities for the rest of her life.

During her forties Emily Dickinson fell in love a second time and, though it was evidently an intense physical sensation, it was a different kind of love from that which she had experienced before. There is no reason to believe that her love for Wadsworth was ever reciprocated or physically enjoyed by so much as an embrace. The second, that shared with Otis Lord, was a mutual love and gave Emily Dickinson some measure of fulfillment — enough at least to satisfy her yearning. Any biographical assessment of the poet must take into account the fact that the two men by whom she was most deeply stirred were both men of intense but controlled emotions; both were impressive, commanding figures; both were intellectually gifted leaders in their respective professions of the ministry and the law; both strongly adhered to the orthodoxies of their chosen fields; and finally, and probably most significant, both were of her father's generation rather than her own. Wadsworth, as a Presbyterian minister, embodied in his sermons and his life the religious doctrines cherished by Edward Dickinson; Lord, her father's closest friend, shared with him the same views about legal and political procedures.

Otis Phillips Lord, a son of the Hon. Nathaniel and Eunice (Kimball) Lord, was born at Ipswich, Massachusetts, in 1812. Though his older brother followed family tradition and attended Harvard College, Otis broke from it and entered Amherst College, whence he was graduated in 1832. Admitted to the bar three years later, he practiced first in Ipswich, removing in 1844 to Salem, where thereafter he resided. In 1843 he married Elizabeth Wise Farley, daughter of Captain Joseph Farley of Ipswich. She was reputed to be beautiful and keenly intelligent. They had no children, but the union, which seems to have been most felicitous, was broken only by her death in December 1877. During the forties and fifties Lord served in the Massachusetts legislature and the State Senate. With the establishment of the Superior Court in 1859, he was appointed an associate justice, in which capacity he served until his elevation to the state Supreme Court in 1875. His Alma Mater recognized his accomplishments in 1869 by conferring on him the honorary degree of Doctor of Laws. The Lords were frequent guests in the Dickinson homestead during Mrs. Lord's lifetime, for Edward Dickinson and the Judge enjoyed agreeing, and disagreeing, on points of politics and law, and were in all ways congenial.

Emily had therefore known the Judge well for some years before Mrs. Lord's death, but all evidence places the development of their affection after 1877. Drafts of Emily's letters, the fair copies of which she undoubtedly sent to him, survive and have been published. The Judge was in a position to offer marriage then, and perhaps did so. He and the nieces who now lived with him were visitors during the late seventies and early eighties in Amherst, where they remained usually for a week at the Amherst House. If he did contemplate marriage, he may have been dissuaded from the idea by the nieces, who appear to have objected. But more likely it was Emily herself who knew that now so major a recasting of her life was impossible. Scraps from her letters imply it. "It is Anguish I long conceal from you to let you leave me, hungry, but you ask the divine Crust and that would doom the Bread . . . I was reading a little Book – because it broke my Heart I want it to break your's. Will you think that fair? I often have read it, but not before since loving you. I find that makes a difference – it makes a difference with all . . . The withdrawal of the Fuel of Rapture does not withdraw the Rapture itself."

The Judge was so seriously ill during 1882 – he was now past seventy – that he felt compelled to resign from the bench. Emily's account of how she received the news of his attack on May first, she wrote to him soon after, when she had been assured that he would recover.

To remind you of my own rapture at your return, and of the loved steps, retraced almost from the "Undiscovered Country," I enclose the Note I was fast writing, when the fear that your Life had ceased, came, fresh, yet dim, like the horrid Monsters fled from in a Dream. Happy with my Letter, without a film of fear, Vinnie came in from a word with Austin, passing to the Train. "Emily, did you see anything in the Paper that concerned us"? "Why no, Vinnie, what"? "Mr Lord is very sick." I grasped at a passing Chair. My sight slipped and I thought I was freezing. While my last smile was ending, I heard the Doorbell ring and a strange voice said "I thought first of you." Meantime, Tom [Kelly – an Irish helper] had come, and I ran to his Blue Jacket and let my Heart break there – that was the warmest place. "He will be better. Dont cry Miss Emily. I could not see you cry."

Her love for the Judge is patent, and the fulfillment for her is in the knowledge that he has desired her. The drama she re-enacts for him is also in character.

Judge Lord died on 13 March 1884, and but few of Emily's close friends now survived. Mr. Bowles, Dr. Holland, Charles Wadsworth — all had gone. Next year Helen Hunt Jackson would go. Emily's own illness had become more severe, confining her for longer intervals to her room or bed. Of those who outlived her, among the closest, there were only Mrs. Holland, the Norcross cousins, and Colonel Higginson. She continued writing her poems till the end, but her great achievement had long since been consummated. Though one senses an anticlimax in the final years, knowing the anguish they had brought, one is grateful for the meed of happiness that Lord's letters and his presence gave her.

Part Two

THE DWELLER IN POSSIBILITY

IV

THE POET AND THE MUSE: Poetry as Art

AS THE STORY can now be reconstructed, sometime during 1858 Emily Dickinson began assembling her poems into packets. Always written in ink, they are gatherings of four, five, or six sheets of letter stationery usually folded once but occasionally single. They are loosely held together by thread looped through them at the spine at two points equidistant from top and bottom. When opened up they may be read like a small book, a fact that explains why Emily's sister Lavinia, when she discovered them after Emily's death, referred to them as "volumes." All of the packet poems are either fair copies or semifinal drafts, and they constitute two-thirds of the whole. For the most part the poems in a given packet seem to have been written and assembled as a unit. Since rough drafts of packet poems are almost totally lacking, one concludes that they were systematically discarded. If the poems were in fact composed at the time the copies were made, as all evidence seems to point, then nearly two-thirds of her poems were created in the brief span of eight years, centering on her early thirties. Her use of packets coincides with the years of fullest productivity.

One of the unanswered questions is what happened to the poems that Emily Dickinson wrote in her youth. Only five can be identified as having been written before her twenty-eighth year, and all of them so slight as to be negligible. The earliest known poem is a valentine dated 4 March 1850, beginning "Awake ye muses nine." It was then the custom for young people to set aside in February a week during which they exchanged valentines, not ornamental printed greetings bought at a stationer's shop, but extravaganzas personally directed toward the individual for whom they were written. Whether they were in prose or verse, they were judged successful in proportion to the comic drollery of their expression. Among her friends, Emily had a reputation for the wit of her concoctions. One forty-line rhyme she sent to Elbridge G. Bowdoin, a young bachelor then practicing law in her father's office. It names "six comely maidens": Emily herself ("she with *curling hair*") and five friends. Can he not choose among them for his true-love? The lines are ornate and vivacious. In 1852 she sent a valentine of the same order to William Howland, another bachelor just beginning the study of law in the same office. Commencing "Sic transit gloria mundi," it is a succession of tag lines and allusions elaborated through seventeen stanzas. Howland retaliated by sending it to the *Springfield Daily Republican*, where it was published on February twentieth with an introductory note saying that the "hand that wrote the following amusing medley . . . is capable of writing very fine things," and expressing the hope "that a correspondence, more direct than this, may be established between it and the Republican." The writer was of course anonymous, but anybody in Amherst who cared to inquire would be told the story. And though valentines were not poetry, still the author of this one, they would judge, was really gifted.

Aside from the two valentines, the only three verses known to be written before 1858 are incorporated in letters. One is to her brother Austin and the others to her friend Susan Gilbert. All are sentimental in tone and commonplace in thought. Pore as one may over the verses in the early packets to identify those which offer clues to earlier associations, only the most tenuous appear. One poem in the handwriting of 1859, "All overgrown with cunning moss," commemorates the death of Charlotte Brontë in 1855. But the very first line indicates the passage of time and leads to the conclusion it was written on the fourth anniversary of her death. The four-stanza poem "I like to see it lap the miles" expresses excitement about the novelty of a steam locomotive. The opening of the two local railroad branches in Amherst in 1853 was something of an event. But the only copy of the poem is a semifinal draft written about 1862, four years after she commenced making her packets, and therefore much later than one would expect to find the poem in packet form were she systematically transcribing early poems into the packets. The poem sent to Sue in 1853, "On this wondrous sea," is in fact duplicated, transcribed into an 1858 packet. Perhaps 1858 was the year of Emily Dickinson's assurance that she was a poet. She certainly must have written poems during her early twenties, but all evidence leads to the conclusion that she later came to feel that most of her earlier verses were spiritless. What she did not destroy she incorporated into the earliest packets, but one suspects that she did not save many. A pattern emerges in her life during the 1850's that seems to have direct bearing on her function first as a writer of verse, then as an artist.

In January 1852 she wrote her brother, who was teaching school in Boston, that there was less gaiety at home with him away, "and we do not have much poetry, father having made up his mind that it's pretty much all real life. Father's real life and mine sometimes come into collision but as yet escape unhurt." A memory ten years later of family differences of opinion about "real life" may have inspired "They shut me up in Prose," with its comment

> Still! Could themself have peeped –
> And seen my Brain – go round –
> They might as wise have lodged a Bird
> For Treason – in the Pound –

Another letter to Austin a year later banteringly acknowledges some attempt of his to write a poem: "And Austin is a poet, Austin writes a psalm. Out of the way, Pegasus. . . Now Brother Pegasus, I'll tell you what it is. I've been in the habit *myself* of writing some few things, and it rather appears to me that you're getting away my patent, so you'd better be somewhat careful or I'll call the police." This letter was written very shortly before she read in the paper of the death of an early friend, Benjamin Franklin Newton, and one surmises that the shock of learning the news delayed her development as a poet, even to the point of drying up the springs of her inspiration, for five years.

Newton was nine years older than Emily Dickinson. Born in Worcester of sturdy parentage, he was taken as a law student into Edward Dickinson's office late in 1847. He had not attended college but he must have had an intelligence and serious-mindedness that the elder Dickinson respected, together with a sensitivity that made him especially dear to Emily during the two years he spent in Amherst. The young men in Edward Dickinson's office were always welcome at his home. Newton was a Unitarian and in Amherst therefore considered somewhat advanced in his thinking. He introduced the Dickinson girls to the writings of the Brontë sisters and the feminist Lydia Maria Child. His presentation to Emily of the 1847 edition of Emerson's *Poems* was made many years before Emerson had become the Concord sage. Newton awakened in her a response to intellectual independence and a delight in literature which later made her call him the "friend who taught me Immortality." In 1850 he returned to Worcester, where he passed his bar examination and set himself up in law practice. He married shortly, but he was already seriously ill, and died of consumption in his thirty-third year.

Ten months after Newton's death she wrote the Reverend Edward Everett Hale, pastor of the Church of the Unity in Worcester, to inquire about Hale's recollections of his former parishioner and his knowledge of Newton's final days. "Mr. Newton," she said, "became to me a gentle, yet grave Preceptor, teaching me what to read, what authors to admire, what was most grand or beautiful in nature, and that sublime lesson, a faith in things unseen, and in life again, much nobler and much more blessed." She adds that after his return to Worcester they had continued their friendship by letter, and three times in later years she alluded to Newton in letters to Higginson. In reply to Higginson's query about her interests and background, she remarked: "When a little Girl, I had a friend, who taught me Immortality – but venturing too near, himself – he never returned. Soon after, my Tutor, died – and for several years, my Lexicon – was my only companion." His reply evidently praised the poems she had previously enclosed, and her next letter in June again alludes to Newton: "Your letter gave no Drunkenness, because I tasted Rum before – Domingo comes but once . . . My dying Tutor told me that he would like to live till I had been a poet, but Death was much of Mob as I could master – then." The place in her heart that Newton filled she mentioned once more to Higginson some fourteen years later: "My earliest friend wrote me the week before he died 'If I live, I will go to Amherst. If I die, I certainly will.'"

Ben Newton was a shaping force in the life that, as she had written her brother just prior to Newton's death, she wished to dedicate to poetry. It thus appears that when Emily Dickinson was about twenty years old her latent talents were invigorated by a gentle, grave young man who taught her how to observe the world, both the seen and the unseen. Their friendship, which always remained on the level of preceptor and pupil, was cut off by his early death. But until the week he died he continued to encourage her hope that she might be a poet, a hope that seemed so sure of realization that she did not hesitate to let Austin share her dream. One recalls her statement that "for several years" after her tutor's death her lexicon was her only companion. Perhaps during the five years after Newton's death she was trying in a desultory manner to fashion verses which she knew were uninspired. Her muse had left the land, and she must await the coming of another. That event seems to have occurred in the late fifties.

In 1858 she gathered some fifty poems into packets. There are nearly one hundred so transcribed in 1859, about sixty-five in 1860, and in 1861 more than eighty. By 1862 the creative drive must have been awesome. During that year she copied into the packets no fewer than three hundred and sixty-six poems, the greater part of them complete and final texts. Whether this incredible number was the product of that year or represents a transcription of earlier worksheet drafts can never be settled by direct evidence, but the quality of tenseness and prosodic skill uniformly present in the poems of 1861–1862 bears scant likeness to the conventionality of subject and treatment in the poems of 1858–1859.

The daemonic force that now possessed her she might or might not be able to master, and she saw the challenge quite literally as a wrestling match. Even as early as 1859 she had used it as a theme in her poem "A little East of Jordan." When Jacob waxed strong, the Angel begged for a respite.

> Not so, said cunning Jacob!
> "I will not let thee go
> Except thou bless me" – Stranger!

The story of how Jacob wrestled with God and was thereby both blessed and disabled she recalled at the conclusion of the scholar-teacher relationship that she maintained with Colonel Higginson for nearly a quarter of a century. In the early spring of 1886, shortly before her death, she wrote Higginson a letter which she intended him to understand would be her farewell message. She comments on her increasing illness and concludes with a note of affectionate remembrance for him and his family: "Audacity of Bliss, said Jacob to the Angel 'I will not let thee go except I bless thee' – Pugilist and Poet, Jacob was correct –" Here the blessing is playfully bestowed by Emily herself, the departing one, an audacious Jacob, who remained to the end a fighter for her way of poetry.

Sometime during 1861, shortly before she initiated her correspondence with Higginson, she describes exactly how the creative impulse takes possession. She is visited, she says, by a "Recordless Company," hosts announced by "Couriers within."

> Alone, I cannot be –
> The Hosts – do visit me –
> Recordless Company –
> Who baffle Key –
>
> They have no Robes, nor Names –
> No Almanacs – nor Climes –

> But general Homes
> Like Gnomes –

> Their Coming, may be known
> By Couriers within –
> Their going – is not –
> For they're never gone –

This kind of visitation persisted so vividly that in 1863 she witnessed to its presence again. This time she names the Host "Immortality."

> Conscious am I in my Chamber,
> Of a shapeless friend –
> He doth not attest by Posture –
> Nor Confirm – by Word –

He takes no liberties and is never troublesome or monotonous. But whether her experience is unique she has no way of guessing.

> Neither if He visit Other –
> Do He dwell – or Nay – know I –
> But Instinct esteem Him
> Immortality –

This Immortality, very much akin to Beauty, is of this world, not of the world to come. There is not the slightest question that she recognized a quality of possession singularly her own, and twice described it during the years of great creativity. By 1861 she had been made aware that such Hosts, whose presence baffled explanation, would bless and isolate her.

Whether the poems in the earliest packets were in fact created in 1858 or in some instances earlier, the truth is that all are written by a person not yet inspired. They are uniformly sentimental, set down by a poet in love with the idea of being in love. Here is one:

> Heart! We will forget him!
> You and I – tonight!
> You may forget the warmth he gave –
> I will forget the light!

When you have done, pray tell me
That I may straight begin!
Haste! lest while you're lagging
I remember him!

Only one poem among them is animated by that catch in the breath which suggests that Emily herself is part of the destiny she seeks to embody in her verses. The enigmatic lines "I never lost as much but twice" speak of being bereft by death of two important friendships, and fearing loss of a third. Leonard Humphrey, a teacher at Amherst Academy whom she had admired, died in 1850. "I am always in love with my teachers," she wrote in her school days. The death of Newton certainly was a loss. The third almost certainly was Charles Wadsworth.

The Reverend Charles Wadsworth was the pastor of the Arch Street Presbyterian Church in Philadelphia from 1850 until April 1862. When Emily and Lavinia returned from a three-week visit in Washington in April 1854, after a visit with their father then serving as a member of Congress, they stopped over in Philadelphia for two weeks early in May as guests of their old school friend Eliza Coleman, whose father, the Reverend Lyman Coleman, had been their principal back in Amherst Academy days. Though there is no record of the event, one supposes that Emily went to hear Wadsworth preach. His reputation as a pulpit orator was equalled only by that of Henry Ward Beecher, and it was unmatched in Philadelphia. A shy, reserved man, who gained his reputation for brilliance from the intensity of his utterance not from histrionics, Wadsworth probably made an unforgettable impression on her. She must have met him at the time. The only certain early fact is that he called on her in Amherst early in 1860, while he was still in mourning after his mother's death in October 1859.

That visit, and another he made briefly twenty years later, in the summer of 1880, are the only two known, and quite possibly the only ones he ever made. But the letters that she wrote after his death on 1 April 1882, state much and imply more. Twice she calls Wadsworth her "closest" or "dearest earthly friend." She says that he was her "shepherd from 'little girl' hood" and that she cannot conjecture a world without him. She wrote Mrs. Holland in October of that year: "It sometimes seems as if special Months gave and took away. August has brought the most to me – April – robbed me most – in incessant instances." A few months later, again writing Mrs. Holland, she is even more pointed. "All other Surprise is at last monotonous, but the Death of the Loved is all moments – *now*. Love has but one Date – 'The first of April' 'Today, Yesterday, and Forever.'"

Over the years she had come to envision him as a "Man of Sorrow," and "a dusk gem, born of troubled waters." The image of him that she carried in her mind is doubtless one that she herself projected. Wadsworth in private life is described as cordial and sunny. Her comments after his death acknowledge that she had been able to learn little or nothing about him as a person or about his children, of whom she makes interested inquiry. The letters that she wrote to him, sent in covering notes to be forwarded by Mrs. Holland, were not so handled to mask a surreptitious romance with a married man. Neither of the Hollands would have cared to be party to such dealings. The method was one that Emily Dickinson adopted for many of her later transactions with the outside world. Except to her sister, who never saw Wadsworth, and to Samuel Bowles, whom she seems to have made her confidant, she mentioned Wadsworth to no one. That fact alone establishes the nature of her emotional turmoil. To name Yahveh is to reveal the unmentionable. The curtains of the Ark of the Covenant must remain drawn.*

* One unsigned, undated letter from Wadsworth, beginning "My Dear Miss Dickenson," [*sic*] survives among papers in the possession of Millicent Todd Bingham, and is published in Mrs. Bingham's *Emily Dickinson's Home* (New York, 1955, pp. 369–372). It is the letter of a pastor concerned that a young woman is suffering anguish of spirit, and expresses a hope that she will confide further if he can lessen her anxiety. Three love letters which Emily Dickinson left in rough draft are also in Mrs. Bingham's collection, and are published in the same volume (pages 422–432). The handwriting is that of late 1861 or early 1862. In them "Daisy" addresses a "Master" for whom she expresses a hopeless love, who "did'nt come to me 'in white,' nor ever told me why." She kept them until her death.

She seems to have sent Bowles a copy of one of her "bridal" poems in 1862.*

> Title divine – is mine!
> The Wife – without the Sign!
> Acute Degree – conferred on me –
> Empress of Calvary!
> Royal – all but the Crown!
> Betrothed – without the swoon
> God sends us Women –
> When you – hold – Garnet to Garnet –
> Gold – to Gold –
> Born – Bridalled – Shrouded –
> In a Day –
> "My Husband" – women say –
> Stroking the Melody –
> Is *this* – the way?

The message which concludes the poem reads: *"Here's* – what I had to 'tell you' – You will tell no other? Honor – is it's own pawn – "

Bowles, who treated Emily in the manner of a devoted older brother, must have replied to the effect: "What goes on here, anyway? What's all this about? What are you getting yourself into?" She appears to have answered in this note:

Dear friend If you doubted my Snow – for a moment – you never will – again – I know –

Because I could not say it – I fixed it in the Verse – for you to read – when your thought wavers, for such a foot as mine –

---

* There is not, and never can be, positive evidence that the copies of the two following poems, with their accompanying notes, were sent to Bowles. The autographs, on identical paper and in the same ink and handwriting, are in the possession of Millicent Todd Bingham, and were collected by her mother Mabel Loomis Todd when the latter was preparing the edition of the Dickinson *Letters* (1894). They were written and sent to someone with whom Emily Dickinson was on terms of confidential intimacy, one whom she looked upon with sisterly affection, whom she addresses with warmth yet deference. Such a relationship was precisely that which she always maintained with Bowles. It does not remotely fit any other.

Then follow these lines:

> Through the strait pass of suffering –
> The Martyrs – even – trod.
> Their feet – upon Temptation –
> Their faces – upon God –
>
> A stately – shriven – Company –
> Convulsion – playing round –
> Harmless – as streaks of Meteor –
> Upon a Planet's Bond –
>
> Their faith – the everlasting troth –
> Their Expectation – fair–
> The Needle – to the North Degree –
> Wades – so – thro' polar Air!

Bowles understood, accepted her as she was, and respected the life she had elected. He wrote Austin in October 1863: "To the [Newman] girls and all hearty thought — Vinnie ditto, — and to the Queen Recluse my especial sympathy — that she has 'overcome the world' — Is it really true that they sing 'Old Hundred' and 'Aleluia' perpetually in Heaven — ask her . . ."

The emotion she was coming to feel by 1860 was the more devastating because it was as genuine as it was hopeless. Wadsworth, now forty-six, was at the zenith of his mature influence, fourteen years married and the head of a family, an established man of God whose rectitude was unquestioned. To her it was a basic necessity that he continue in all ways to be exactly the image of him that she had created. For her he must be both immediate and afar, acutely desired yet renounced, a physical being to be seen and touched if only by handclasp after long intervals, yet a counselor to be longed for and reached by letter. The fantasy that Wadsworth proposed an elopement has no basis in fact, and controverts all that is known of the psychology of either. The "bridal" and renunciation poems have meaning when interpreted as a part of Emily Dickinson's lifelong need for a preceptor, a muse whom she could adore with physical passion in her imagination. Viewed otherwise they make no sense at all. The extent to which Wadsworth realized the nature of her adoration can only be conjectured. He was a cosmopolitan minister of ready perceptions who long since had acquired the knowledge how to deal with exactly such problems. She certainly never made demands on him that were other than proper for a minister of the gospel to meet, though there was undoubtedly an affinitiveness in their emotional response to spiritual and intellectual issues.

Her eagerness after his death to learn from his lifelong friend, James D. Clark, details of his life and personality is a measure of his reticences as a person, however responsive he must have been professionally. Though he himself wrote verses on occasion, one doubts that their communications touched upon poetry or that he was aware that her creative energies stemmed from the spell which he had unaccountably induced. One imagines that she gained her inspiration from the relationship that her imagination projected, but that her letters to him, however emotional they may have been in matter touching upon the soul's affections, were somewhat disembodied. When she initiated her correspondence with Higginson in April 1862, she turned to one who could in fact serve as a critic of her verse, which by this time she was writing as if she were pursued by Furies. She soon came to call Higginson her "preceptor" and her "safest friend," and quite literally he became both to her. Though at first their letters were exchanges of ideas, the correspondence soon came to include news about family and friends. But Higginson never was what Newton had once been, and Wadsworth overpoweringly became: the source of inspiration itself. By 1860 she had already been writing a greatly increased proportion of poems that reveal firm texture and a deepened purpose: "Just lost, when I was saved," "I shall know why – when Time is over," and "At last, to be identified." It is in the two years following that the floodgates opened and she wrote with inspired creativeness. Whereas Newton had awakened her to a sense of her talents, Wadsworth as muse made her a poet.

A crisis in Emily Dickinson's life seems to have been precipitated by Wadsworth's acceptance of a call to the Calvary Church in San Francisco in December 1861. The two notes to Bowles seem to follow this event. Wadsworth had been considering the call for some time, and probably mentioned the fact to Emily Dickinson as long before as September. It is the plausible conjecture usually set forth to explain two sentences in her second letter to Higginson. Having spoken of the friend who taught her immortality, she goes on to say: "Then I found one more – but he was not contented I be his scholar – so he left the Land." And she gave as the primary reason for writing poetry at all: "I had a terror – since September – I could tell to none – and so I sing, as the Boy does by the Burying Ground – because I am afraid."

To Emily Dickinson, Wadsworth's departure was heart-rending. The distance was so appallingly vast that his removal, permanent as far as anyone knew, seemed to her a living entombment. He might as well be in Timbuctoo or Van Diemen's Land, or any of the places that to her were far locations. He sailed on May first and arrived on the twenty-fourth. It is at this time that she began to dress entirely in white, adopting, as she calls it, her "white election." The name Calvary now first appears in her poems. In 1862 alone she used it nine times, and once again in 1863, always in verses charged, like this, with intense emotion.

> That I did always love
> I bring thee Proof
> That till I loved
> I never lived – Enough –
>
> That I shall love alway –
> I argue thee
> That love is life –
> And life hath Immortality –
>
> This – dost thou doubt – Sweet –
> Then have I
> Nothing to show
> But Calvary –

There is no other place name, in the entire range of her poetry, used anywhere nearly so often or with such personal association. She speaks of herself as Queen of Calvary. Grieving for a lost lover or for one renounced, she recalls "old times in Calvary." In the poem "Title Divine is mine," as "Empress of Calvary" she is "Born – Bridalled – Shrouded – in a Day." She had revealed herself frankly enough to Bowles so that he called her "the Queen Recluse." In 1863 she began one poem "Where Thou art – that is Home/ Cashmere or Calvary – the Same . . ./ So I may come."

A mere listing of first lines of some of the highly emotional poems of "marriage" and renunciation that were written late in 1861 or early 1862 shows the extent to which her overwrought feelings were poured out. None of them was ever sent to a correspondent; all remained privately her own.

I got so I could hear his name

What would I give to see his face

Wild nights, wild nights

I dreaded that first robin so

I had the glory – that will do

I felt my life with both my hands

The day that I was crowned

Although I put away his life

How sick to wait

I live with him, I see his face

Mine by the right of the white election

I cannot live with you – that would be life

In one packet alone, written early in 1862, are these:

I know that he exists, somewhere in silence

I envy seas whereon he rides

I tend my flowers for thee, bright absentee

At least to pray is left, is left

Is bliss then such abyss

After great pain a formal feeling comes

It will be summer eventually

'Twas the old road through pain

As far as eye could peer, Wadsworth's function as preceptor must perforce cease.

It is significant that in June 1869, after Wadsworth's return from California had been publicly announced, Emily Dickinson invited Colonel Higginson to Amherst. "Of our greatest acts we are ignorant. You were not aware," she says, "that you saved my Life. To thank you in person has been since then one of my few requests." Higginson could know part of what she meant — that he had given her private audience for her poems. But he could not know, as she of course was aware that he could not, in just what way he had provided a release from the tensions and preserved her sanity. Two very unfinished worksheet drafts, which have every evidence of having been written in 1868 or 1869, express a mood of jubilation. One deserves to be quoted:

Oh Sumptuous moment
Slower go
That I may gloat on thee —
'Twill never be the same to starve
Now I abundance see —

Which was to famish, then or now —
The difference of Day
Ask him unto the Gallows led —
With morning in the sky

By 1870 Wadsworth was again established in Philadelphia, in another church where he continued as pastor until his death. The crisis in Emily Dickinson's life was over. Though nothing again would wring from her the anguish and the fulfillment of the years

1861–1865, she had yet several years ahead to write verses, few by comparison, but many among them that embody her art at its serenest.

It seems to have been in 1860 that Emily Dickinson made the discovery of herself as a poet and began to develop a professional interest in poetic techniques. Her thoughts about poetry and the function of the poet can be gleaned from her own poems and from occasional snatches in her letters. Her writing techniques were self-taught. She did not follow traditional theories, but developed her own along highly original lines. Though she could write excellent prose, easy, clear, unmannered, the fact is that she thought in poetry. By 1858, at ease with the way of life she had elected and found congenial, she had begun to let the form of her verse derive from the images and sensations that she wished to realize. Her growth as an artist can be followed by way of her experiments in prosody. She worked steadily at her trade during 1860 and 1861, and by 1862, when she feared that the loss of her muse would overwhelm her, she had mastered her craft.

Although writers of free verse acknowledge a debt to Emily Dickinson, she wrote in fact almost nothing which today would be called *vers libre*, that is, cadenced verse, as distinguished from that which is metrical or rhymed. Her first attempt to do so in 1862, "Victory comes late," seems to have been her last, for it evidently convinced her that such a form was not the medium which best transmitted her mood and ideas. There are a variety of ways to gain controlled liberty. She herself, she felt, needed rhyme and meter. To her contemporaries, and to most critics at the time her poems were first published, her seemingly unpatterned verses appeared to be the work of an original but undisciplined artist. Actually she was creating a new medium of poetic expression.

Basically all her poems employ meters derived from English hymnology. They are usually iambic or trochaic, but occasionally dactylic. They were the metric forms familiar to her from childhood as the measures in which Watts's hymns were composed. Copies of

Watts's *Christian Psalmody* or his collection of *The Psalms, Hymns, and Spiritual Songs* were fixtures in every New England household. Both were owned by Edward Dickinson and are inscribed with his name. The latter is bound in brown sheepskin, and bears his name in gold on the cover. Musical notations for proper rendition accompany each song, and the meter is always named. Introductions set forth an explanation of how effects may best be achieved, and discuss the relative advantage of one meter over another for particular occasions. Emily Dickinson's own experimentation went beyond anything envisioned by the formal precisionists who edited Watts's hymns and songs, but the interesting point is that she did not have to step outside her father's library to receive a beginner's lesson in metrics.

The principal iambic meters are these: *Common Meter*, alternately eight and six syllables to the line; *Long Meter*, eight syllables to the line; and *Short Meter*, two lines of six syllables, followed by one of eight, then one of six. Each of these meters has properly four lines to the stanza, so that their syllabic scheme goes thus: *CM*, 8, 6, 8, 6; *LM*, 8, 8, 8, 8; *SM*, 6, 6, 8, 6. Each may also be doubled in length to make eight-line stanzas. Each may also have six lines to the stanza. Thus *Common Particular Meter* has the metric beat 8, 8, 6, 8, 8, 6; and *Short Particular Meter*, 6, 6, 8, 6, 6, 8. Other popular arrangements were *Sevens and Sixes* (7, 6, 7, 6) and *Sixes*. The principal trochaic meters are *Sevens*, *Eights and Sevens*, *Eights and Fives*, *Sevens and Fives*, *Sixes and Fives*, and *Sixes*. Of the dactyls, which were arranged principally in *Elevens*, *Elevens and Tens*, and *Tens and Nines*, Emily Dickinson used almost exclusively the last named when she chose it as the meter for an entire poem. But she used the dactyl sparingly and almost always as an adjunct to one of the other meters.

It is significant that every poem she composed before 1861 — during the years she was learning her craft — is fashioned in one or another of the hymn meters named above. Her use of Long Meter was sparing, for, as her hymn-book instructions pointed out, it tends to monotony. A very large proportion of her poems are in

Common Meter. Next in order are Common Particular, and Sevens and Sixes, in equal proportion. She chose Short Meter for relatively few, but achieved with it some of her best effects. Her trochaics are chiefly Eights and Sevens, and Eights and Fives — a new meter, introduced into hymnody toward the mid-nineteenth century.

The meters so far named by no means exhaust the variations that hymnodists were coming to use, but one need not believe that Emily Dickinson's later combinations of Nines and Sixes, Nines and Fours, or Sixes and Fours derived from a model. By the time she came to use them she was striking out for herself. Indeed her techniques would be of scant interest had she set down her stanzas with the metric regularity of her models, and enforced her rhymes with like exactness. Her great contribution to English prosody was that she perceived how to gain new effects by exploring the possibilities within traditional metric patterns. She then took the final step toward that flexibility within patterns which she sought. She began merging in one poem the various meters themselves so that the forms, which intrinsically carry their own retardment or acceleration, could be made to supply the continuum for the mood and ideas of the language. Thus iambs shift to trochees, trochees to dactyls, and on occasion all three are merged.

At the same time she put into practice her evident belief that verse which limits itself to exact rhyme is denied the possible enrichment that other kinds can bring. Her pioneering is here too in the new order erected on old foundations. She felt no more bound to one kind of rhyme than she did to one meter. She should have realized that she was charting a lonely voyage, and in some degree she did, but her independent nature gave her self-assurance. Her way of poetry was to prove far lonelier than she expected, for it denied her in her own lifetime all public recognition. The metric innovations might have been tolerated, but in her day no critic of English verse would have been willing to accept her rhymes. Milton had proved that English verse could be great with no rhyme at all. No one in 1860, reader or critic, was ready to let it be supple and varied.

Custom decreed exact patterns and exact rhymes in English poetry, with concessions to a spare use of eye rhymes (*come-home*). Her grounding in French and in classical literature, however elementary or imperfect, must have assured her that English custom had no preëmptive sanction. She enormously extended the range of variation within controlled limits by adding to exact and eye rhymes four types that poets writing in English had never learned to use expertly enough to gain for them a general acceptance: identical rhymes (*move-remove*), vowel rhymes (*see-buy*), imperfect rhymes [identical vowels followed by different consonants] (*time-thine*), and suspended rhyme [different vowels followed by identical consonants] (*thing-along*). These rhymes she selected at will, singly or in combination, and she carried her freedom to the utmost limit by feeling no compulsion to use one rhyming pattern in a poem any more than she felt constrained to use a single metric form. Thus in a poem of three quatrains the rhyme in the first stanza may be exact for the second and fourth lines, suspended in the second stanza for lines three and four, and conclude in the third stanza with imperfect rhymes for the first and fourth lines. The wheel horses of her stanzas are always the final lines, whether the poem is written as a series of quatrains or as a combination of stanza patterns.

Within this structure she was seldom wayward, nor did she have to be, for it gave her ample room for variety of mood, speed, and circuit. Examination of the intent of a poem usually reveals a motive for the variations. Sometimes she seems to have felt, as the reader does today, that a poem was unskilfully realized, for she abandoned a great many such efforts in worksheet draft. In the past editors have published her finished poems side by side with texts created from unfinished worksheets. Thus imperfectly realized poems have been given a status which the poet never thought them to have. The level of the poet's achievement is raised when such unfinished labors are not weighed in.

One of the very earliest poems to adopt combinations of patterns is the following, written in 1858.

I never told the buried gold
Upon the hill – that lies –
I saw the sun – his plunder done
Crouch low to guard his prize.

He stood as near
As stood you here –
A pace had been between –
Did but a snake bisect the brake
My life had forfeit been.

That was a wondrous booty –
I hope twas honest gained.
Those were the fairest ingots
That ever kissed the spade!

Whether to keep the secret –
Whether to reveal –
Whether as I ponder
"Kidd" will sudden sail –

Could a shrewd advise me
We might e'en divide –
Should a shrewd betray me –
Atropos decide!

The metric and rhyme shifts are many and seem to be deliberate. The first two stanzas, in Common Meter, are followed by a third in Sevens and Sixes. The fourth, beginning in line two, shifts to trochaic Sixes and Fives, with which the poem concludes in stanza five. The rhymes are exact in the first, second, and last stanzas; imperfect in the third, and suspended in the fourth. There are internal exact rhymes in the first and third lines of stanzas one and two. The poem survives in two fair copies, and in both she has deliberately arranged the second stanza in five lines.

The variations are studied and so elaborate that they distract the reader. She appears to be describing a brilliant sunset, and is undecided whether to share the "secret" or not. The structural form when she narrates the facts of the event is exact in meter and rhyme.

Both shift uncertainly as she points out her own indecision. It is not an important poem. The imagery is imprecise and the intent not clearly realized. The poet is still a tyro, but such skill as the poem has — and unmistakably it bears her stamp — lies in the blending of the form with the mood.

The poem below, also written in 1858, is an accomplishment of the first order. The skills she was developing are more easily handled in two quatrains than in five.

> I never lost as much but twice,
> And that was in the sod.
> Twice have I stood a beggar
> Before the door of God!
>
> Angels — twice descending
> Reimbursed my store —
> Burglar! Banker — Father!
> I am poor once more!

The first stanza is written in Common Meter with a catalectic third line — that is, it lacks a final syllable. The device was one that she developed with uncanny skill to break the monotony of exact regularity. The second stanza is a trochee in Sixes and Fives. Here the metric irregularity is balanced by exact rhymes. The exactness of the rhymes gives finality to the terseness of the thought. The metrical shift turns the resignation of the first statement into the urgency of the second.

Sometime about 1860 she wrote this:

> Just lost, when I was saved!
> Just felt the world go by!
> Just girt me for the onset with Eternity,
> When breath blew back,
> And on the other side
> I heard recede the disappointed tide!
>
> Therefore, as One returned, I feel,
> Odd secrets of the line to tell!
> Some Sailor, skirting foreign shores —

Some pale Reporter, from the awful doors
Before the Seal!

Next time, to stay!
Next time, the things to see
By Ear unheard,
Unscrutinized by Eye –

Next time, to tarry,
While the Ages steal –
Slow tramp the Centuries,
And the Cycles wheel!

It is arranged in several metric patterns, altered so rapidly that no single form predominates. The final short stanza alternates iambs with trochees, to give the effect of applying brakes, and thus brings the slow tramp of the centuries to a halt. The final words of each stanza effect a rhyme, and most of the rhymes are exact. In the first stanza the mating rhyme word is in the line preceding, and in the second it is separated by three intervening lines. In the last two stanzas it is at the point normally expected, that is, in the alternating line. There are further rhymes in the first two stanzas, exact, vowel, and suspended. This elaborateness is shaped throughout to the mood the poem intends to convey, a mood of awe in facing the fact that any vision of immortality seen by mortals is a mirage. The structure of the poem allows great latitude in tempo and shading. The poem is one of her best early attempts to create by way of letting the form be shaped by the mood. The method requires a skill which cannot be taught, but must be guided by instinctive taste. She herself did not win through to full success on all occasions. But the universal pleasure this poem has given is some measure of its fulfillment.

A very large number of poems written during 1860 and 1861 experiment with new models. She used much the same technique as that in the poem above when she created "At last, to be identified," evidently with intent likewise to suggest breathlessness. In 1860 she also wrote the expertly realized "How many times these

low feet staggered." It is the quiet meditation of one who gazes upon
the face and form of a dead friend. The metrics are coldly regular.
The hovering rhyme of the first stanza becomes exact in the remaining two stanzas. The artistry lies in the vivid concreteness of the
detail, set forth with great restraint. On the privacy of this moment
no rhetorical extravagance is allowed to obtrude.

The new order of love poems is exemplified by this.

> I'm 'wife' – I've finished that –
> That other state –
> I'm Czar – I'm 'Woman' now –
> It's safer so –
>
> How odd the Girl's life looks
> Behind this soft Eclipse –
> I think that Earth feels so
> To folks in Heaven – now –
>
> This being comfort – then
> That other kind – was pain –
> But why compare?
> I'm 'Wife'! Stop there!

Suspended rhymes join each pair of lines except the last, which
conclude the poem with exact rhymes. Each stanza has its individual metric form, allied to but not identical with the others. The
Sixes and Fours of the first stanza become Sixes in the second. In
the third, the Sixes are paired, as are the Fours.

The rhythmic exactness of "Did the Harebell loose her girdle/
To the Lover bee" is as studied as the irregularity in "What is
'Heaven,'" written at the same time. The poem below is an excellent example of both her concern with and indifference to rhyme
and metrical exactness.

> I taste a liquor never brewed –
> From Tankards scooped in Pearl –
> Not all the Frankfort Berries
> Yield such an Alcohol!

Inebriate of Air – am I –
And Debauchee of Dew –
Reeling – thro endless summer days –
From inns of Molten Blue –

When "Landlords" turn the drunken Bee
Out of the Foxglove's door –
When Butterflies – renounce their "drams" –
I shall but drink the more!

Till Seraphs swing their snowy Hats –
And Saints – to windows run –
To see the little Tippler
From Manzanilla come!

The poem uses Common Meter, but the regularity is broken in two ways. The third lines of the first and fourth stanzas are both catalectic, and the rhymes of those stanzas are imperfect. These variations unquestionably were deliberate, for they are typical of her modifications of traditional forms. Yet the only surviving manuscript of the poem is a semifinal draft on which she offers alternative readings for two lines. For line three she suggests: "Not all the vats upon the Rhine," and for the final line: "Leaning against the sun." The first alternative, if adopted, would supply the missing half-foot; the second would create an exact rhyme. We cannot infer from the fact that the suggested changes exist that she would have adopted them in a fair copy. She frequently did not do so. There are instances where two fair copies, each sent to a friend, show like indifference to rhyme and metric patterns. One may hazard the opinion that her choice in any event would have been determined by her preference for one image rather than another, not by a desire to create exact meter and rhyme.

She must have been groping too for ways of expression that said things as she individually wished to say them. Certain of her idiosyncrasies in language and grammar become obtrusive when sprinkled too freely, but they are characteristic and often very effective. Her use of what seems to be the subjunctive mood comes first to mind. Yet the fact is that perhaps it is not subjunctive at all in the sense of being grammatically an optative or volitive or potential mood. "Only love assist the wound" may be read as "Only love can assist the wound." But more probably, because more in line with the way her mind worked, she means "Only love does assist the wound." If this is her meaning, then what at first seems to be a subjunctive mood might better be called a continuing or universal present indicative. She recognized her dilemma in the line "Beauty — be not caused — It Is." As a suggested change she offers "is" for "be," as though she were uncertain whether the substantive sense was too unidiomatic to convey her idea clearly. But even the first reading cannot be called subjunctive, for it does not denote a contingency, but expresses an idea as fact. She was trying to universalize her thought to embrace past, present, and future. Such is her intent in the following instances, which could be multiplied greatly, so often does her mind explore universals.

> Nature — the Gentlest Mother is . . .
> And when the Sun go down —
> Her Voice among the Aisles
> Incite the timid prayer

> The One who could repeat the Summer Day . . .
> When Orient have been outgrown —
> And Occident — become Unknown —
> His Name — remain —

> The Robin is the One
> That interrupt the Morn

This concept of language is allied to but different from that which prompted her to cultivate elliptical phrases as a way of paring words that complete sentences grammatically but do not communicate. Of course on occasion she cut too deeply into the quick of her thought because she truncated her predication to the point where readers must perpetually grope for meaning. But where her intent is realized, the attar becomes haunting and unforgettable.

She had the precedent of her greatest teacher, Shakespeare, for an occasional reversal of nominatives and objectives: "That Mush-room – it is Him," or "As blemishless as her." She preferred *lain* to *laid* as a past participle. Certain colloquialisms such as *don't* for *doesn't* she used because familiarity with them was natural to her ear and tongue: "It don't sound so terrible – quite – as it did." Others like *heft* for *weight* one suspects she chose because the Anglo-Saxon quality of words always pleased her: "There's a cer-tain Slant of light/ . . . That oppresses like the Heft/ Of Cathe-dral Tunes," or "The Brain is just the weight of God –/ For – Heft them – Pound for Pound . . ." Learned words irritated her. In the poem in which she says she prefers "star" to "Arcturus" she com-ments:

> I slew a worm the other day –
> A "Savan" passing by
> Murmured "Resurgam" – "Centipede"!
> "Oh Lord – how frail are we"!

Her use of the dash as end-stop punctuation often replaces con-ventional commas and periods. Within lines it frequently is with-out grammatical function, but is rather a visual representation of a musical beat. The emotion is thus conveyed in the poem begin-ning:

> Sweet – safe – Houses –
> Glad – gay – Houses –

Such dashes become an integral part of the structure of her poetry. Her portmanteau words she took seriously: overtakelessness, re-pealless, failless. In the lines "Better an ignis fatuus/ Than no illume at all" she tries to revive the Elizabethan experimentation in making verbs function as nouns. All of this is a sort of informed waywardness, used with sufficient restraint and affection for lan-guage as never to offend even when it does not illuminate. In language as in thought she seems to be asking to take two steps ahead if on occasion she falls back one.

The power of words to evoke a mood is the subject of half a dozen poems. "A Word made Flesh is seldom/ And tremblingly partook," she remarks, adding, "A Word that breathes distinctly/ Has not the power to die." She knew that the will to select words was not always within her conscious power.

> Shall I take thee, the Poet said
> To the propounded word?
> Be stationed with the Candidates
> Till I have finer tried –

But the word came unsummoned. "Not unto nomination/ The Cherubim reveal."

Her intent in "I like a look of agony" and "To die takes just a little while" is to make the reader experience an emotion. She wishes to re-create in words two moments of suffering, yet to stand outside the anguish and by a kind of ironic indifference to deepen the inherent compassion.

> I like a look of Agony,
> Because I know it's true –
> Men do not sham Convulsion,
> Nor simulate, a Throe –
>
> The Eyes glaze once – and that is Death –
> Impossible to feign
> The Beads upon the Forehead
> By homely Anguish strung.

The metric pattern is formally exact, relieved from constraint by the use of vowel and suspended rhymes. In the poem "There's a certain Slant of light" she reversed the method to gain the same end.

At some period late in 1861, when she came to know of Wadsworth's impending departure, she was evidently panic-stricken. She had become increasingly skillful and productive. Would she ever in fact be able to write again? Public announcement that Wadsworth would soon conclude his duties as pastor of the Arch Street

Church was made on 15 March 1862. He remained six weeks longer before the congregation yielded and granted his dismissal, and a week later he and his family were on the high seas. The effect on Emily Dickinson during the early spring seems to have been quite different from what she expected. Her creative abilities, rather than decreasing, enormously multiplied. Yet even as this was happening, she seems to have been deeply apprehensive lest each day's composition be the last. Such an eventuality did not occur, and she was so sure of her achievement that she was willing to write Higginson, enclosing four of her best poems, to ask a professional man of letters to tell her what he thought of them. She was led to seek his guidance for two reasons. She feared that the loss of her muse would prevent further accomplishment and hoped that the inspiration might in some unpredictable way be forthcoming through the new association. Secondly, she was fully aware that her verses deserved an audience. The story of her friendship with Higginson will be told shortly. At this point one need say only that the impending departure of Wadsworth is closely tied into her compulsion to write Higginson during that April. Her comment to Higginson when she invited him to Amherst seven years later that he had saved her life, and that since then to thank him in person had been one of her few requests, cannot be lightly passed over.

Emily Dickinson's prosodic expertness was fully realized in 1862. The exquisite "She lay as if at play" is one of her poems on the theme of death. The brevity of the little life is paralleled by the short trimeter-dimeter lines. The rhymes are delicate interplays of suspended, imperfect, and exact sound arrangements. She marshals her vowels, both in rhymes and within the lines, in such a way as to suffuse with light such a poem as "I had no time to Hate," and especially this below.

> "Why do I love" You, Sir?
> Because –
> The Wind does not require the Grass
> To answer – Wherefore when He pass
> She cannot keep Her place.

Because He knows – and
Do not You –
And We know not –
Enough for Us
The Wisdom it be so –

The Lightning – never asked an Eye
Wherefore it shut – when He was by –
Because He knows it cannot speak –
And reasons not contained –
– Of Talk –
There be – preferred by Daintier Folk –

The Sunrise – Sir – compelleth Me –
Because He's Sunrise – and I see –
Therefore – Then –
I love Thee –

The shift from iambic to a trochaic beat in the final line is expertly maneuvered. The authority of "After great pain, a formal feeling comes" derives from the technical skill with which the language is controlled. As she always does in her best poems, Emily Dickinson makes her first line lock all succeeding lines into position.

After great pain, a formal feeling comes –
The Nerves sit ceremonious, like Tombs –
The stiff Heart questions was it He, that bore,
And Yesterday, or Centuries before?

The Feet, mechanical, go round –
A Wooden way
Of Ground, or Air, or Ought –
Regardless grown,
A Quartz contentment, like a stone –

This is the Hour of Lead –
Remembered, if outlived,
As Freezing persons, recollect the Snow –
First – Chill – then Stupor – then the letting go –

The heaviness of the pain is echoed by *bore, wooden, quartz, stone, lead*. The formal feeling is coldly ceremonious, mechanical, and stiff, leading through chill and stupor to a "letting go." The stately pentameter measure of the first stanza is used, in the second, only in the first line and the last, between which are hastened rhythms. The final two lines of the poem, which bring it to a close, reëstablish the formality of the opening lines. Exact rhymes conclude each of the stanzas.

Emily Dickinson's impulse to let the outer form develop from the inner mood now begins to extend to new freedoms. Among her poems composed basically as quatrains, she does not hesitate to include a three-line stanza, as in "I rose because he sank," or a five-line stanza, as in "Glee, the great storm is over." On some occasions, to break the regularity in yet another way or to gain a new kind of emphasis, she splits a line from its stanza, allowing it to stand apart, as in "Beauty – be not caused – It Is," and "There's been a Death, in the Opposite House." Sometimes poems beginning with an iambic beat shift in succeeding stanzas to a trochaic, to hasten the tempo, as in "In falling timbers buried." It is the year too when she used her dashes lavishly.

This is also the time when she wrote two love poems that employ sexual imagery with unabashed frankness.

> Wild Nights – Wild Nights!
> Were I with thee
> Wild Nights should be
> Our luxury!
>
> Futile – the Winds –
> To a Heart in port –
> Done with the Compass –
> Done with the Chart!
>
> Rowing in Eden –
> Ah, the Sea!
> Might I but moor – Tonight –
> In Thee!

When Colonel Higginson and Mrs. Todd were selecting verses for the Second Series of *Poems*, in 1891, he wrote her saying: "One poem only I dread a little to print — that wonderful 'Wild Nights,' — lest the malignant read into it more than that virgin recluse ever dreamed of putting there. Has Miss Lavinia any shrinking about it? You will understand & pardon my solicitude. Yet what a loss to omit it! Indeed it is not to be omitted." The poem was included. The second goes much further in its metric pointedness.

> How sick – to wait – in any place – but thine –
> I knew last night – when someone tried to twine –
> Thinking – perhaps – that I looked tired – or alone –
> Or breaking – almost – with unspoken pain –
>
> And I turned – ducal –
> *That* right – was thine –
> *One port* – suffices – for a Brig – like *mine* –
>
> Our's be the tossing – wild though the sea –
> Rather than a Mooring – unshared by thee.
> Our's be the Cargo – *unladen – here* –
> Rather than the "spicy isles –"
> And thou – not there –

The water imagery is conspicuous in both poems, but the metrics of the second derives from the mood. The slow regularity of the beginning is speeded up at the end of the second stanza. The third stanza opens with a panting dactyl that slows to a quiet measure, shortened, in the last line, to two feet. The imagery throughout is unmistakably concrete.

This is manifestly erotic poetry. From what experience was she enabled to give these sensations an artistic creation? With what intent did she write the poems? Answers to such questions may be hidden, but their concealment cannot prevent the knowledge that any creation is a true statement of something. She wrote the poems and she transcribed them fair into her packets. When Higginson answered her first letter and commented on the poems she had enclosed, he must have felt that her metric liberties gave her verse some resemblance to that of Walt Whitman, and evidently asked if she had read any of Whitman's poetry, because she replied: "You speak of Mr Whitman – I never read his Book – but was told that he was disgraceful." There is much that one can never know about the human heart. But one dares hazard a guess about one basic difference in the natures of Walt Whitman and Emily Dickinson. Had the shy spinster been confronted with the implications of her artistic achievement, she would have accepted the fact with stoic resignation, whereas Whitman would have expressed pleasure at his success.

The misery occasioned by Wadsworth's departure for California in 1862 did in fact mature her. In that and in succeeding years she wrote with a vision which gives her rank as a philosophical poet. It was much later that she sketched the genre pictures of aspects of life about her. At this point she was exploring within herself, the "undiscovered continent," to determine the relationship between man and both worlds, the seen and the unseen. It is impossible that she could have written earlier such poems as "The Soul selects her own Society," "She lay as if at play," "I died for Beauty," "We play at Paste," and others of like quality. Two written at this time repay a study of their rhyme and their metric organization.

> 'Twas a long Parting – but the time
> For Interview – had Come –
> Before the Judgment Seat of God –
> The last – and second time
>
> These Fleshless Lovers met –
> A Heaven in a Gaze –
> A Heaven of Heavens – the Privilege
> Of one another's Eyes –
>
> No Lifetime set – on Them –
> Appareled as the new
> Unborn – except They had beheld –
> Born infiniter – now –

Was Bridal – e'er like This?
A Paradise – the Host –
And Cherubim – and Seraphim –
The unobtrusive Guest –

Its theme is supernal love. Parted in life, the lovers meet before
the judgment seat for the last "and second" time, and there wed
with Paradise as host and the angels as guests. The tone is wistful
because the poet envisions consummation only after "a long Parting." The first stanza is in Common Meter. The poem gains speed
thereafter by employing Short Meter. Suspended rhymes run
through all stanzas, and thus the mood of incompletion is echoed
in the verse structure. The theme of the second is identical, but
the mood is very different.

Of all the Souls that stand create –
I have elected – One –
When Sense from Spirit – files away –
And Subterfuge – is done –
When that which is – and that which was –
Apart – intrinsic – stand –
And this brief Tragedy of Flesh –
Is shifted – like a Sand –
When Figures show their royal Front –
And Mists – are carved away,
Behold the Atom – I preferred –
To all the lists of Clay!

Common Meter is used throughout, and thus the pace is un-
altered. The rhymes, in alternate lines, are exact. The mood of the
poem is one of jubilant assurance because the election already has
been made. Here, as in the first, the prosodic structure helps shape
the mood and give it firmer texture.

Emily Dickinson's new-found artistic and spiritual maturity is
made strikingly evident by comparing two poems which express
attitudes about the problems of daily living. In 1859 she had thought
of them in terms of mathematical sums, and had concluded that

new problems always seem larger than those with which we have previously dealt.

> Low at my problem bending,
> Another problem comes –
> Larger than mine – Serener –
> Involving statelier sums.
>
> I check my busy pencil,
> My figures file away.
> Wherefore, my baffled fingers
> Thy perplexity?

Six years later her perceptions have deepened and the language in which she gives them form has sharpened.

> The Missing All – prevented Me
> From missing minor things
> If nothing larger than a World's
> Departure from a Hinge –
> Or Sun's extinction, be observed –
> 'Twas not so large that I
> Could lift my Forehead from my work
> For Curiosity.

Clearly she had found herself.

V

MY SAFEST FRIEND: Renunciation

FROM A LITERARY POINT OF VIEW, April 15, 1862 is
the most significant date in Emily Dickinson's life, for, enclosing a
card on which she had penciled her name, and four poems, she
wrote a professional author to inquire whether her verses "breathed."
She was then thirty-one years old. At the time she despatched her
letter to Thomas Wentworth Higginson, he was living in Worcester where he had recently resigned his Unitarian pulpit to devote
himself entirely to writing and lecturing. Born in Cambridge, Massachusetts, in 1823, the youngest of the ten children of Stephen
and Louisa (Storrow) Higginson, he was a descendant, through
both lines, of Bay Colony forebears. His father, a prosperous mer-
chant, was bursar of Harvard College, the institution with which
Higginsons had been associated from the date of its founding. After
being graduated from Harvard second in his class at the age of
seventeen, young Higginson taught school for two years, and then,
with no fixed purpose except to increase his reading background,
he returned to the college as a "resident graduate" for three years
more. At that point he was admitted to the Senior class of the
Divinity School and was graduated with it in 1847. Devoted
throughout his long life to liberal causes, he now associated himself
with the "disunion abolitionists," those whose radical views led
them to prefer dissolution of the Union unless slavery were abol-
ished. In September 1847 he became pastor of a Unitarian church
in Newburyport, and in the same year married his cousin Mary
Elizabeth Channing, to whom he had been engaged for five years.
Liberal as the Unitarianism of his day might be, his outspoken

utterances on social and political issues had within two years alien-
ated many of his more conservative parishioners, who felt that
his participation in acts of violence on behalf of fugitive slaves did
more credit to his heart than his judgment. At the time of his resignation he wrote his mother that he was glad to be released "from
a life which did not content me." The profession was the only one
for which he had been trained, and in the spring of 1852 he accepted the call of a "Free Church" in Worcester, where he remained until 1861. But his interest was not in parish work. Twice
in 1856 he went West to engage directly in antislavery ventures,
accounts of which he sent as letters to the New York *Tribune* and
published later that year as a tract entitled *A Ride Through Kansas*.

The truth is that he spent increasingly more time away from his
church, for he was beginning to win a reputation as social reformer
on the lyceum platform. By 1861 he had come to the conclusion
that he did not have a true call to the ministry, and his decision to
leave it was final. His association with other publicists was congenial, and his prestige as a lecturer and writer gave him confidence
that his talents should be used to promote social reform and give
direction to literary expression.

Emily Dickinson dared bring herself to Higginson's attention
because she had just read the "Letter to a Young Contributor" that
he had written as the lead article in the *Atlantic Monthly* for April.
It was practical advice for beginners, with emphasis on smoothness
of style, and avoidance of prolixity and high-flown language.
"Charge your style with life," he said, and the remark is one she
echoed back to him in her first letter: "Are you too deeply occupied
to say if my Verse is alive?" One sentence in his article she would
quote back to him many years later, and it is a clue to the reasons
why she now felt emboldened to write him: "Such being the majesty of the art you presume to practice, you can at least take time
before dishonoring it." His "Letter" happened to appear in print at
exactly the moment, and be absorbed by exactly the person, to give
historical significance to an utterance intrinsically commonplace.
It drew responses and specimens of verse, all of which, he wrote

James T. Fields, the *Atlantic* editor, were "not for publication." Though he judged the poetry of Emily Dickinson unfit to publish, he was fascinated by it, if somewhat embarrassed. He immediately answered Miss Dickinson's letter, asking her to send more poems, inquiring her age, her reading, her companionships, and requesting further details about her writing.

She replied at length, withholding her age, but responding to his other inquiries with a candor that reveals the depth of her need for literary companionship. One sentence in this second letter surely misled Higginson as it has all others since the letter was published. "I made no verse –," she says, "but one or two – until this winter – Sir –," and cryptically hints as a reason for her new diversion certain recent emotional disturbances. But the truth evidently she could not admit even to herself. The remark is a classic of understatement. When she wrote that letter, she had in fact composed no fewer than three hundred poems, and was bringing others into being at a rate which would double the number by the end of the year. She was writing to Higginson, not as a novice, but as an artist. She could perhaps justify her remark by believing that "until this winter" extended backward several months, and that the poems written earlier than 1861, before her art had matured, on the whole constituted "no verse." To some extent she was showing what Higginson later termed her "naive adroitness." But the statement she made raises a fascinating and probably unanswerable question. When does a person deny semi-casual work and lay claim to genius? In this instance, though it is no answer, one can say only that Emily Dickinson posted her letter of inquiry on April fifteenth. In any event she had selected as a first offering what she considered to be representative of her best art. Would he believe, as she seems to have had self-confidence enough to hope, that her verses lived and breathed?

The clearest answer to the questions can be given by discussing the four poems that she enclosed in her first letter, set down exactly as Higginson received them. To us who have the advantage of afterthought they are by no means the work of a beginner. They are in fact the creations of an artist who understands that form is inherent in the created object.

> Safe in their Alabaster Chambers –
> Untouched by Morning –
> And untouched by Noon –
> Sleep the meek members of the Resurrection,
> Rafter of Satin – and Roof of Stone –
>
> Grand go the Years,
> In the Crescent above them –
> Worlds scoop their Arcs –
> And Firmaments – row –
> Diadems – drop –
> And Doges – surrender –
> Soundless as Dots,
> On a Disc of Snow.

What embarrassed Higginson about such lines was his inability to classify them. They might be "beautiful thoughts and words," as he later referred to some verses that she sent to him, but they were not poetry. She would shortly come to know that he thought them, as he was to do all his life, "remarkable, though odd," but "*too delicate*," as he phrased it to a friend, " – not strong enough to publish." One can understand much of his perplexity as it arose by way of the unorthodoxy in her form and language, and realize too that his search for words to express his quandary was thoughtful, but the phrase "too delicate" seems curiously inept.

Just why had Emily Dickinson selected Higginson as the critic on whom to rely? Why not Bryant or Lowell or Emerson, or some other writer or editor of the first rank? There must have been a large element of chance in the selection, from which, once she had made it, she felt she could not retreat. She was clearly on the point of making some kind of a decision, and had Higginson's article not been written, her election might have fallen on another. As we know, she needed both a critic and a "preceptor," and thought perhaps she had found both in him. He was known as a liberal thinker, interested in the status of women in general and women writers in particular. She genuinely admired his writing. He was also, it seemed to her, a member of a socially established family that took pride in plain living and high thinking, and the Dickinsons felt instinctively drawn to such society. She could not know that Higginson had let no opportunity slip in cultivating his wide literary and social acquaintanceships, and that he was rather skillful at name-dropping, in his letters at any rate. She may have considered such public figures as Bryant and Lowell, but rejected them as too awesome. It was common knowledge that Emerson's praise of Whitman had been effusive. Since she judged Whitman to be "disgraceful," she may have questioned Emerson's taste.

Higginson was in fact a representative mid-nineteenth-century American critic, whose tastes and judgments were neither more nor less discerning than those of most of his contemporaries. Nor was his estimate other than would have been made by the fraternity of literary appraisers. Only a Sainte-Beuve can stand above or outside traditional proprieties, or recognize a new art form and help the artist win a public. Such critics are rare in any civilization, and in 1862 America was young and culturally self-conscious. To appreciate the formidable handicap, one needs only to recall Wagner's struggle, in Europe, during the same years, to win acceptance of his leitmotiv as an operatic form.

Higginson's impression after he had pondered the "Alabaster" poem was that it lacked form. It was imperfectly rhymed and its metric beat spasmodic. He was trying to measure a cube by the rules of plane geometry. The poem is in dimensions he was not equipped to estimate. Emily Dickinson has devised a melodic pattern, controlled by key words, wherein the parts express the whole. The stately pace of the first stanza intimates the vast leisure of the dead. *Alabaster*, in the opening line, is the first control: an inanimate substance, it is cold, hard, white, and translucently smooth. The altered meter in the second stanza is more rapid and less regular. Time passes in a world of successive, but living, generations. *Crescent*, a word associated with the pallid moon, suggests the great arc through which the years wheel majestically above and around the noiseless dead until Resurrection Day. Years are reckoned by the fall of dynasties. The final word, *snow*, completes the cycle of ideas. It is cold, white, silent. But it introduces a completely new dimension. Unlike alabaster it is soft, like a blanket, and the reader is suddenly conscious that the motion of the second stanza has become gently rhythmical, as though a cosmic Mother Nature were rocking her children, now soundlessly asleep.

The second poem that he encountered, assuming that he read them in such order, was this:

> I'll tell you how the Sun rose –
> A Ribbon at a time –
> The Steeples swam in Amethyst –
> The news, like Squirrels, ran –
> The Hills untied their Bonnets –
> The Bobolinks – begun –
> Then I said softly to myself –
> "That must have been the Sun"!
> But how he set – I know not –
> There seemed a purple stile
> That little Yellow boys and girls
> Were climbing all the while –
> Till when they reached the other side,
> A Dominie in Gray –
> Put gently up the evening Bars –
> And led the flock away –

This poem progresses at a lighthearted gait, like a nursery rhyme. The meter is a subtle blending of Sevens, Sixes, and Eights, and the poet chose to make the rhymes exact after the first quatrain. The theme deals with the living, not the dead. Dawn and sunset are personified, and the motion is that of human activity: swimming, running, climbing. The colors are airy; first the bluish-violet streaks of dawn (amethyst), then the varigated hues implied in "Bonnets." There is the sound of bobolinks. By sunset the purple and yellow fade into grey. The flocks are in pastoral care and we are led to feel that they will be returned next day in good order.

The third poem represents, not the regular motion of the sun, but the zigzag of a bee.

> The nearest Dream recedes – unrealized –
> The Heaven we chase,
> Like the June Bee – before the School Boy,
> Invites the Race –
> Stoops – to an easy Clover –
> Dips – evades – teases – deploys –
> Then – to the Royal Clouds
> Lifts his light Pinnace –
> Heedless of the Boy –
> Staring – bewildered – at the mocking sky –
>
> Homesick for steadfast Honey –
> Ah, the Bee flies not
> That brews that rare variety!

The theme — that we mock ourselves if we think happiness lies in chasing an imagined heaven — is matched by the aberration of the dipping, evading bee. The form, though in fact organized, suggests aimless disorganization. In the first stanza rhyme is abandoned after line four, and as the stanza concludes, the eye is directed up — but into vacancy. Vowel rhymes bring the second stanza into formal relation with the first, but otherwise the form like the thought is juxtaposed, not blended, with the preceding ten lines. The stanza remains, as the theme states about idle dreamers, in lonely isolation.

The fourth enclosure deals in thirty words with the development of the artist. In technical virtuosity, though not in amplitude, it is the most fascinating of the group. Could it be that Emily Dickinson chose to send it as a way of sounding Higginson out, of letting him see, if he had the power she hoped he might, that she had passed the stage of "practicing sands"?

> We play at Paste –
> Till qualified, for Pearl –
> Then, drop the Paste –
> And deem ourself a fool –

The Shapes – though – were similar –
And our new Hands
Learned *Gem*-Tactics –
Practicing *Sands* –

No language could say more directly that the writer looks back
upon the work she produced four or five years ago and finds it
trifling. (Did she toss most of it into the wastebasket?) But the
shapes used to create it were, she knows, similar in form. To be sure
they were, but how different the current accomplishment! Here she
uses three varieties of rhyme: identical, exact, and suspended. The
idea of the poem juxtaposes the tyro and the artist, and the form does
likewise for the two stanzas. The alternate iambic dimeter-trimeter
regularity of the first stanza is abandoned in the second, where the
meter follows its own convention, striking out in a new direction.
Most interesting are the two final lines. The thought of line seven
concerns the artist whose craft is learned; that of line eight, the
learner. It can hardly be a matter of chance that the metric patterns
of the two lines enforce the thought by reversing the beat thus:
ᴜ – – ᴜ / – ᴜᴜ –. Emily Dickinson wrote many inferior poems, as
indeed all poets of first rank have done. But the four that she offered
Higginson in her first letter are not among them.

After Emily Dickinson's death, when Higginson with Mrs.
Todd's help was preparing the Second Series of *Poems* in 1891, he
published an article in the October *Atlantic Monthly* to give the
public a foretaste of verses to be issued in November. It reproduced
several of the letters he had received, and some of the poems, among
them "We play at Paste," and "The nearest Dream recedes unreal-
ized." Of the first he said that it "comprises in its eight lines a truth
so searching that it seems a condensed summary of the whole experience of a long life." The fatuousness of the remark is beside
the point. The fact is that he never came to have the slightest concept of what Dickinson's artistic achievement consisted, not even
when he timidly sponsored publication. His comment on the other
poem is of such a nature as to raise serious doubt whether he even

understood it. "Then came one which I have always classed among the most exquisite of her productions, with a singular felicity of phrase and an aerial lift that bears the ear upward with the bee it traces." He quotes it, and continues: "The impression of a wholly new and original poetic genius was as distinct on my mind at the first reading of these four poems as it is now, after thirty years of further knowledge; and with it came the problem never yet solved, what place ought to be assigned in literature to what is so remarkable, yet so elusive of criticism. The bee himself did not evade the schoolboy more than she evaded me; and even at this day I still stand somewhat bewildered, like the boy." He still, even as he consents to edit it, does not really think it is poetry! The evasion was never Emily Dickinson's.

Returning to the year 1862, we can perhaps understand why he could not possibly give preceptorial aid. He literally did not understand what he was reading. It is inconceivable that, had he actually believed that he was dealing with an original genius, he would have advised against publication and on the grounds, as he had put it, that the poems were "not strong enough."

The first weeks of this letter exchange were critical in Emily Dickinson's literary life. She sensed the quality of her art and believed, as she had good reason to believe, that her apprenticeship was over. She did not write the distinguished judge of good writing merely to tease him, should he beg permission to find a publisher for her poems, by coyly refusing to release them from her bureau drawer. She asked for coaching as the finished artist turns to a noted conductor to ask what he suggests as a final polish. Higginson told her in effect that she knew very little about singing.

The second letter to Higginson, written ten days later on April twenty-fifth, enclosed further poems, as he had asked her to do. There were three: "There came a Day at Summer's full," "Of all the Sounds despatched abroad," and "South Winds jostle them." Like those in her first letter they were selected for their range of theme and prosodic variety. This letter makes the statement that "Two Editors of Journals came to my Father's House, this winter —

and asked me for my Mind — and when I asked them 'Why,' they said I was penurious — and they, would use it for the World." Would the statement perhaps delicately tell Higginson that others were competing with any possible advice he might wish to give about the medium of publication? One supposes that the request came from Samuel Bowles and Dr. Holland. The very fact that her personal ties with them were close would be an incentive to seek the judgment of a disinterested referee. The fact is that within the year two of her poems had been published in the *Republican,* anonymously to be sure, and the second of the two just six weeks before she wrote Higginson.

Her realization that Higginson the critic had nothing to offer her would come shortly. But even before she wrote to him she had been made aware of the liberties that editors took with one's text, to smooth a rhyme and make a "sensible" metaphor, with the result that the printed object before one were better disowned. Her poem "I taste a liquor never brewed" had appeared in the "Original Poetry" column of the *Republican* in May 1861. As she had written the first stanza, it read:

> I taste a liquor never brewed —
> From Tankards scooped in Pearl —
> Not all the Frankfort Berries
> Yield such an Alcohol!

But the editors wanted a rhyme and they produced a version that could never, by any stretch of the imagination, have been hers.

> I taste a liquor never brewed,
>   From tankards scooped in pearl;
> Not Frankfort berries yield the sense
>   Such a delirious whirl.

At the time she wrote Higginson she does not seem to be trying to avoid publication as such; she is inquiring how one can publish and at the same time preserve the integrity of one's art. The most recently published poem, in the same newspaper, was an earlier version of "Safe in their Alabaster Chambers." It too had been altered.

Since none of Higginson's earlier letters survive, the nature of his comments must be inferred from her replies, which in some degree explain her aesthetic theory. Her third letter of June seventh is especially important, since it establishes both her convictions about her art and her need of Higginson's friendship in spite of his total lack of discernment as to her purpose as artist. He had suggested that, since her rhymes were imperfect or casually dropped in, she might better give them up entirely. She says that she "could not drop the Bells whose jingling cooled my Tramp." For Higginson a rhyme, or indeed a poem for that matter, was something to be produced as you get water from a tap. Emily Dickinson was incapable of an analysis of her techniques. She knew that she had in large degree mastered them, and she knew by June what Higginson thought of them. But even if she had been able to explain, she would never have affronted the kindly friend who was willing to respond to her appeal with a sincere if bewildered understanding. Her own certainties are positively implied in two sentences, each written as a separate paragraph. "You think my gait 'spasmodic' – I am in danger – Sir. You think me 'uncontrolled' – I have no Tribunal."

The crucial sentences are buried in the middle of the letter. "I smile when you suggest that I delay 'to publish' – that being foreign to my thought, as Firmament to Fin." But it is the sentence which follows that makes her acquiescence in his verdict poignant. "If fame belonged to me, I could not escape her – if she did not, the longest day would pass me on the chase – and the approbation of my Dog, would forsake me – then. My Barefoot Rank is better." Those are not the words of a person who courts obscurity. They well from the integrity and self-knowledge of one who is willing to lose battles in her lifetime so that in after-years the war will be won. She asks him to receive whatever she may send, promising never to impose on his good will. She concludes: "But will you be my Preceptor, Mr Higginson?" This outpouring of spirit is already a personal cry, a psychological necessity, and it is uttered in the face of his rejection of her work as art. As one trained in pastoral care, he early sensed the personal need, but to his dying day he could never resolve the dilemma his literary judgment created. She had elected, by June 1862, a poetic obscurity in her lifetime, by Higginson's verdict.

The poems enclosed in Emily Dickinson's second letter to Higginson are of the same order of excellence as those in the first. Precisely what he had said about the first group can be inferred only to the extent that she comments: "Thank you for the surgery – it was not so painful as I supposed." She goes on to say that she is sending more, as he requested, "though they might not differ." She then adds: "While my thought is undressed I can make the distinction, but when I put them in the Gown, they look alike and numb." What she means is that when she gathers them in one envelope, to be critically reviewed by a professional judge, she feels the usual fright experienced by an actor awaiting his initial cue. One reasonably suspects that her selection this time bore some relation to his opinions expressed about the first group. This was the briefest:

> South Winds jostle them –
> Bumblebees come –
> Hover – Hesitate – Drink, and are gone –
> Butterflies pause – on their passage Cashmere –
> I, softly plucking,
> Present them – Here –

It is one of the earliest of the many "flower poems" she would write all her life, verses intended to accompany the surprise of a blossom. She felt the same assurance about its quality as poetry as she had felt about the earlier poems she sent, because she made at one time or another no fewer than four fair copies of it. Written in 1859, it was incorporated in an early packet as two quatrains. A year later she gave it the metric arrangement of the copy she sent to Higginson. It rhymes exactly only in lines four and six, but there are hovering rhymes throughout. The meter too suggests the hesitating motion of a butterfly. The next poem sets the wind in motion.

Of all the Sounds despatched abroad,
There's not a Charge to me
Like that old measure in the Boughs –
That phraseless Melody –
The Wind does – working like a Hand,
Whose fingers Comb the Sky –
Then quiver down – with tufts of Tune –
Permitted Gods, and me –

Inheritance, it is, to us –
Beyond the Art to Earn –
Beyond the trait to take away
By Robber, since the Gain
Is gotten not of fingers –
And inner than the Bone –
Hid golden, for the whole of Days,
And even in the Urn,
I cannot vouch the merry Dust
Do not arise and play
In some odd fashion of it's own,
Some quainter Holiday,
When Winds go round and round in Bands –
And thrum upon the door,
And Birds take places, overhead,
To bear them Orchestra.

I crave Him grace of Summer Boughs,
If such an Outcast be –
Who never heard that fleshless Chant –
Rise – solemn – on the Tree,
As if some Caravan of Sound
Off Deserts, in the Sky,
Had parted Rank,
Then knit, and swept –
In Seamless Company –

Though its fingers comb the sky, it remains a fleshless chant, a
caravan moving through the deserts of sky in ranks that part, then
seamlessly knit together. The motion is carried into the stillness of

the tomb, where the merry dust rises to play. Stanzas one and three are identically rhymed in their second and fourth and last lines with a close "e." Elsewhere rhymes occur by chance and in varying forms. The vowels rhythmically alternate between open and close sounds. Words suggesting sounds and motion predominate, echoing back and forth like an antiphonal choir.

The third enclosure, a love poem, was the seven-stanza "There came a Day at Summer's full," which since its publication in 1890 has been one of the best-known poems. Structurally it is the most conventional of the three, as it is in image and idea. She perhaps selected it because she believed that Higginson would sympathetically respond to it.

His letter in reply clearly did two things. It gave her substantial praise, but made plain his certainty that she could not expect to publish the kind of poetry she had been sending to him. In his opinion a person simply could not be possessed by a glee "among my mind," or have a thought go "up my mind," or talk of "a hay," when everyone knows that *hay* is a collective noun. The fact that she "almost always grasped whatever she sought," as he acknowledged after her death, was not enough. She did so by an unforgivable "fracture of grammar and dictionary on the way." In her third letter she accepts the praise by saying: "I have had few pleasures so deep as your opinion," and meets the verdict he passed down by disclaiming any intention to publish. But had that been so in April? It may be significant that seven weeks had been allowed to pass before the third letter was written. It may also be significant that she wrote this poem sometime during 1862:

> Myself was formed – a Carpenter –
> An unpretending time
> My plane – and I, together wrought
> Before a Builder came –
>
> To measure our attainments –
> Had we the Art of Boards
> Sufficiently developed –He'd hire us
> At Halves –

116

> My tools took Human – Faces –
> The Bench, where we had toiled –
> Against the Man – persuaded –
> We – Temples build – I said –

Higginson was a builder who had the "Art of Boards" very well developed, but she could not be persuaded that he knew how to erect temples.

There is no question but that in later years she set herself firmly against the idea of publishing. The note to Sue in 1861 during their exchange of ideas on the "Alabaster" poem has the sentence expressing hope that someday she could make Sue and Austin "proud – sometime – a great way off." She would not expect them to be proud merely that she wrote poetry. She wants them to have the opportunity of being proud that she will have become a name. On March 1, 1862, the same poem appeared unsigned in the *Springfield Daily Republican,* and on that same day Sue wrote her an excited note: "*Has girl read Republican?* It takes as long to start our Fleet as the Burnside." (General Burnside had captured Roanoke Island a few weeks earlier.) What plans had been laid to start "our" fleet? The tone of Sue's question certainly implies that Emily will be pleased to see the poem in print.

She could defer to Higginson's judgment because she believed his opinion represented the best literary judgment that she could find. She knew that it confirmed the appraisal of Mr. Bowles and Dr. Holland. They admired her originalities, but like Higginson they did not believe that she really wrote poetry. Even so, she did not have the slightest intention of altering her way of writing, since it expressed the way her senses received their impressions.

To be sure, in a technical sense an audience of one is a public, and she could thenceforth send poems to Higginson and others. But with the exception of those to Higginson and Sue, the number of poems that thus gained a hearing is a miniscule fraction of the whole. Her growing preoccupation with the subject of fame is a striking characteristic of the poems written between 1862 and 1865. The dedication to her art had begun before she wrote to Higginson.

It was a dedication that led to renunciation of fame in her lifetime and, as the wellsprings of her creativeness dried up after 1865, to increasing seclusion. There is strong evidence, on the other hand, that she came to think of herself as a public name in the fact that six times, between the years 1866 and 1872, she signed letters to him simply "Dickinson." And this she did once again in 1885, when writing another author, Helen Hunt Jackson.

By seeing things in the way others see them, or in the way we are all expected to see them, one may achieve a certain public recognition for one's talents. Since her destiny must be followed according to her individual self-discoveries, she had no choice but to let the fame come late.

> Some – Work for Immortality –
> The Chiefer part, for Time –
> He – Compensates – immediately –
> The former – Checks – on Fame –

The vision deepens in 1863, and is expressed with deft clarity:

> Fame of Myself, to justify,
> All other Plaudit be
> Superfluous – An Incense
> Beyond Necessity –
>
> Fame of Myself to lack – Although
> My Name be else Supreme –
> This were an Honor honorless –
> A futile Diadem –

Fame may be justified if one retains one's honor, but the thought that she could win it only at the cost of being classified during her lifetime as the composer of "beautiful thoughts and words" sometimes rankled. "Fame is a fickle food," she wrote disparagingly,

> Whose crumbs the crows inspect
> And with ironic caw
> Flap past it to the
> Farmers Corn
> Men eat of it and die

When she wrote that "publication is the auction of the mind of man," she was in part writing an apology for the isolation that she must endure because she had no other choice. A subterranean vehemence runs through the poem.

> Publication – is the Auction
> Of the Mind of Man –
> Poverty – be justifying
> For so foul a thing
>
> Possibly – but We – would rather
> From Our Garret go
> White – Unto the White Creator –
> Than invest – Our Snow –
>
> Thought belong to Him who gave it –
> Then – to Him Who bear
> It's Corporeal illustration – Sell
> The Royal Air –
>
> In the Parcel – Be the Merchant
> Of the Heavenly Grace –
> But reduce no Human Spirit
> To Disgrace of Price –

In all the long history of poetry, as Emily Dickinson well knew, the association of publication and "price" has been negligible if not nonexistent. The motive for such assocation here lies in a reaction to praise for wrong reasons, or for praise so carefully hedged that one felt limp with exasperation. The words "poverty," "futile," "compensate," and "justify" are conspicuous in the poems on the subject of fame.

By 1865 she had won a measure of resignation.

> The first We knew of Him was Death –
> The second – was – Renown –
> Except the first had justified
> The second had not been.

Renown comes after death. She here uses "justified" in the traditional theological sense of one made acceptable to God and worthy of salvation. The use, in all ways, is apt.

In February 1866 her poem "The Snake" appeared anonymously in the columns of the *Republican*. The supposition is that Bowles, who had seen and admired it, thought that Emily had approved its publication, although Sue evidently supplied the copy. In a manuscript that Emily gave Sue, the first stanza is rendered:

> A narrow Fellow in the Grass
> Occasionally rides –
> You may have met him? Did you not
> His notice instant is –

In the *Republican* the meaning is altered by a punctuation shift:

> You may have met him – did you not,
> His notice instant is.

Already sensitive to editorial correction, Emily now felt helpless. In March she enclosed a clipping of "The Snake" in a note to Higginson, protesting: "Lest you meet my Snake and suppose I deceive it was robbed of me – defeated too of the third line by the punctuation. The third and fourth were one – I had told you I did not print – I feared you might think me ostensible." Torn between a desire to share and the knowledge that public sharing could never be accomplished on her terms, she will never again be entirely reasonable in matters touching upon the publication of her poems.

There had been two reasons for writing to Higginson in the first place; the ostensible one has been discussed. The second reason was that she desperately needed to establish an association which would combine a vista into the world of letters with some kind of guardianship. She wanted to find someone to whom she could "recite," yet who affinitively was "safe." It is much more than coincidence that her search for safety was undertaken at the time Wadsworth was preparing for his departure to San Francisco. His going altered the pattern of her life, but it also gave purpose to her central interest. Though he still remained her muse, Higginson became her mentor. Higginson communicated his own serenity, and in ways which he instinctively understood, gave her the therapy she sought. By the summer of 1862, when he had convinced her that her poems were not for publication in her lifetime, but had established himself as the friend who would respond as often as she needed to call upon his aid, she reached a new level of artistic growth. Even before she wrote Higginson the literary critic, she knew all about Higginson the minister, the friend of liberal causes and women's rights. Their relationship stabilized during the summer of 1862 exactly as she hoped it would do and for her a new and very important bond was forged. Thenceforth she could think of fame in terms of success sublimated. "Success is dust."

This June letter reveals the depth of the craving. In matters touching upon his criticism of her poems, she is politely unsubmissive. She thanks him for the "justice" of his observations, knowing the uselessness of explication, the egregiousness of explaining to a judge why his verdict had been reached before he had considered all the evidence. And yet she continues: "If I might bring you what I do — not so frequently to trouble you — and ask you if I told it clear — 'twould be control, to me — The Sailor cannot see the North — but knows the Needle can — The 'hand you stretch me in the Dark,' I put mine in, and turn away — I have no Saxon, now." Language, she means, fails her. It is this letter that asks him to be her "preceptor."

In his October 1891 *Atlantic* article Higginson makes clear that he early came to see that her need for him lay outside her wish for criticism: ". . . on my side an interest that was strong and even affectionate, but not based on any thorough comprehension; and on her side a hope, always rather baffled, that I should afford some aid in solving her abstruse problem of life." His perceptions on this point were admirably clear, and his willingness to play the game by her rules, to give the help she needed by simply replying as a friend to her letters, is to Higginson's everlasting credit.

The temptation to ridicule Higginson for his obtuseness in

dealing with the poetry, both in her lifetime and after, has proved irresistible to all Dickinson biographers, and not without reason. Yet his situation was unique. A normally discriminating traditionalist, he was sought out by a "wholly new" order of craftsman who demanded to be his pupil. She pleaded for his criticism even after both of them knew that she did not mean what she said when she urged him to give it. Even more insistent on that subject is her fourth letter, written in July, with such entreaties as these:

I am happy to be your scholar, and will deserve the kindness, I cannot repay.

If you truly consent, I recite, now.

Will you tell me my fault, frankly as to yourself, for I had rather wince, than die. Men do not call the surgeon, to commend – the Bone, but to set it, Sir, and fracture within, is more critical. And for this, Preceptor, I shall bring you – obedience – the Blossom from my Garden, and every gratitude I know . . .

To thank you, baffles me – Are you perfectly powerful? Had I a pleasure you had not, I could delight to bring it.

This is the first letter she signed "Your Scholar," the practice that she later made customary. Higginson may have laughed indulgently when he found his pupil asking the question: "Are you perfectly powerful?" It is witty, but one doubts that he saw, either then or later, that he had been scored on.

No poems had been enclosed in the third letter, though one was incorporated in the text, the expert and appealing "As if I asked a common Alms." She placed four poems in her fourth letter: "Of Tribulation – these are They," "Your Riches taught me poverty," "Some keep the Sabbath going to Church," and "Success is counted sweetest." This is also the letter in which she told him that her business is circumference. In the first named poem she misspelled *ankle* as *ancle,* and at the bottom of the sheet called his attention to her error. In his 1891 *Atlantic* article, Higginson says with expansive indulgence: "It would seem that at first I tried a little, — a very little — to lead her in the direction of rules and traditions; but I fear it was only perfunctory, and that she interested me more in her —

so to speak — unregenerate condition. Still, she recognizes the endeavor. In this case, as will be seen, I called her attention to the fact that while she took pains to correct the spelling of a word, she was utterly careless of greater irregularities. It will be seen by her answer that with her usual naïve adroitness she turns my point." Naïve? She had indeed done so, for now it was a game to be enjoyed, as Charles Lamb remembered about Mrs. Battles' whist, for its rigors. In August she replied, enclosing two poems this time: "Before I got my eyes put out," and "I cannot dance upon my Toes," both sparkling verses. She writes: "Are these more orderly? I thank you for the Truth. . . I think you call me 'Wayward.' Will you help me improve? . . . You say I confess the little mistake, and omit the large — Because I can see Orthography — but the Ignorance out of sight — is my Preceptor's charge."

Several paragraphs of chatter intervene. At one point she seems to be answering a comment to the effect that she should try to get out and meet people oftener, because she says: "Of 'shunning Men and Women' — they talk of Hallowed things, aloud — and embarrass my Dog. . . I think Carlo would please you — He is dumb, and brave." The sentences are carefully spaced because offence would have been intolerable to her. But she clearly finds the game exhilarating. She now brings her artillery up for the final shot: "I shall observe your precept — though I dont understand it, always." She knew that Higginson, who delighted in the society of women, might not respond instantly, but one imagines she hoped that he would never know he was so directly hit. Removed from their context, the sentences sound far more abrupt than in fact they are, for the letter moves easily through a variety of thoughts, all entertaining but associated only by her own chain of consciousness. This sentence is typical: "When much in the Woods as a little girl, I was told that the Snake would bite me, that I might pick a poisonous flower, or Goblins kidnap me, but I went along and met no one but Angels, who were far shyer of me, than I could be of them, so I hav'nt that confidence in fraud which many exercise."

From 1863 to 1869 she wrote Higginson an average of but one

letter a year. He himself was much occupied, for in the summer of 1862 he had helped to raise and drill a company of Massachusetts volunteers, and in November was about to start for the front when he was offered the colonelcy of the first Negro regiment in the Union army. He accepted the command of the 1st South Carolina Volunteers, and remained with his regiment until May 1864, when complications resulting from a slight battle wound compelled him to relinquish his command. Meantime Mrs. Higginson, in delicate health, had moved to Newport, Rhode Island, where the Colonel joined her and they continued to reside until her death thirteen years later.

Receiving no reply to her August letter, and unaware of Higginson's preoccupation with affairs, Emily Dickinson wrote tersely in October: "Did I displease you, Mr Higginson? But wont you tell me how?" He took occasion to write her during the winter, for she replied in February, signing herself "Your Gnome," probably because he had made some remark to the effect that she wrote aphoristic or gnomic verses. "I trust you may pass the limit of Wars, and though not reared to prayer – when service is had in Church, for Our Arms, I include yourself." With this letter she enclosed "The Soul unto itself."

In the autumn of 1863 began the trouble with her eyes, which bothered her to such an extent that by late April 1864 she was compelled to spend some weeks under a physician's care, in Boston. She took occasion during May to write Higginson, inquiring about his injury and telling about herself. Though forbidden the use of a pen, she continued to write poems: "I work in my Prison and make Guests for myself." The condition of her eyes made imperative her return to Boston for a similar period of time in the following year, and some eighteen months elapsed before she next wrote him, in January 1866, to announce the demise of her great dog Carlo and to enclose the poem "Further in Summer than the Birds," one of her notable achievements. "Carlo died," the letter reads. "Would you instruct me now?" Whether or not the Colonel offered instruction, he certainly urged her in his reply to be his guest at a Boston

literary gathering. In declining she asked: "Is it more far to Amherst? You would find a minute Host but a spacious Welcome."
Again she reminds him that he is her tutor. "If I still entreat you
to teach me, are you much displeased? I will be patient – constant,
never reject your knife. . ." Soon thereafter Higginson renewed
his invitation, with the same result: "Might I entreat you as my
Guest to the Amherst Inn? When I have seen you, to improve will
be better pleasure because I shall know which are the mistakes."
It was a most harmless game, which both seemed to enjoy. Two
years elapsed before the next brief note, which merely enclosed a
poem or two, and again asked for instruction.

The year 1867 remains mysterious. Neither by direct nor in-
direct evidence is there one poem or letter or one event in Emily
Dickinson's life that can be surely fitted into it. Though 1868 is
not such a total blank, it too seems to have been a year of limited
activity. By 1869 vitality suddenly returns. The full tide of her
letter exchange with Higginson begins soon thereafter, and during
the decade of the seventies she wrote him more than forty letters.
In May 1869, acknowledging some verses she had sent him, he said
to her: "Sometimes I take out your letters & verses, dear friend, and
when I feel their strange power, it is not strange that I find it hard
to write & that long months pass. I have the greatest desire to see
you, always feeling that perhaps if I could once take you by the
hand I might be something to you; but till then you only enshroud
yourself in this fiery mist & I cannot reach you, but only rejoice in
the rare sparkles of light." He continues:

It is hard [for me] to understand how you can live s[o alo]ne, with
thoughts of such a [quali]ty coming up in you & even the companionship of your dog withdrawn. Yet it isolates one anywhere to think beyond
a certain point or have such luminous flashes as come to you – perhaps
the place does not make much difference.

You must come down to Boston sometimes? All ladies do. I wonder
if it would be possible to lure you [to] the meetings on the 3rd Monday
of every month at Mr. [Sa]rgent's 13 Chestnut St. at 10 am – when
somebody reads [a] paper & others talk or listen. Next Monday Mr.

Emerson [rea]ds & then at 3½ P.M. there is a meeting of the Women's [Cl]ub at 3 Tremont Place, where I read a paper on the [Gre]ek goddesses . . . You see I am in earnest . . . I have a right to invite you & you can merely ring & walk in.

It is puzzled and earnest and straightforward and almost wistful — as if he felt something in their relationship which he wished he could grasp was escaping him. Of course psychologically she would have found it impossible to go, but one can think of no situation that she would relish in her imagination more keenly than attending the meeting to hear the Colonel discourse on Greek goddesses. It was three years later that she sent him the third and fourth lines only of this poem:

> The Show is not the Show
> But they that go —
> Menagerie to me
> My Neighbor be —
> Fair Play —
> Both went to see —

She used them to conclude a letter that thanks him for a "lesson."

I will study it though hitherto

> Menagerie to me
> My Neighbor be.

The remark must have puzzled Higginson, as almost certainly it was intended to do. But she so obviously enjoys her game with her preceptor, and so often resorts to private associations to play it, that one may be pardoned for associating the two lines with her memory of an invitation to a literary gathering which she did not attend.

The long letter that she wrote in reply to his invitation to Boston insistently renews her own invitation that he come to Amherst. She ends it by saying what he must always have believed: that her correspondence with him, however desultory it might have been during the past seven years, had in fact carried her through years of almost insupportable distress. To thank him in person now became imperative.

In mid-August 1870, Colonel Higginson found that his travel plans made an overnight stop at the Amherst Inn convenient. He wrote to inquire if she would be at home and could receive him. She replied that she would "be at Home and glad." The meeting of the two on the sixteenth is historically important, for it made possible the sole existing record of a conversation with Emily Dickinson. Her literary friendships were few, and Higginson was the only man of letters she ever requested to see. By now almost totally withdrawn from physical contacts with the outside world, she seems to have found that even this meeting demanded all her nervous fortitude. Higginson's diary entry for the day refers to the call as a "remarkable experience, quite equalling my expectations." He sensed that the encounter might be significant beyond anything he could then foretell, for he made a report of it in two letters to his wife, one written that evening, the other on the day following. The accounts are observant and detached.

He arrived in Amherst that Tuesday at two in the afternoon and remained until nine on the following morning. He says that he called on President Stearns and on a Mrs. Banfield, but he probably did so late in the day, since President Stearns could not find a janitor to open the building Higginson wished to see. He notes that he saw Emily Dickinson twice, and met her father in the morning. One infers that he made a brief courtesy call before his train departure at nine.

He found Amherst a pleasant country town, "unspeakably quiet in the summer afternoon." Arriving at the Dickinson home, a "large country lawyer's house, brown brick, with great trees and a garden," he sent up his card and waited in the cool, dark parlor. "A step like a pattering child's in entry & in glided a little plain woman with two smooth bands of reddish hair . . . in a very plain & exquisitely clean white piqué & a blue net worsted shawl. She came to me with two day lilies, which she put in a sort of childlike way into my hand & said 'These are my introduction' in a soft frightened breathless childlike voice — and added under her breath Forgive me if I am frightened; I never see strangers & hardly know what I say — but she talked soon & thenceforward continuously — & deferentially — sometimes stopping to ask me to talk instead of her — but readily recommencing. Manner between Angie Tilton & Mr. Alcott — but thoroughly ingenuous & simple which they are not & saying many things which you would have thought foolish & I wise — & some things you would have liked. I add a few over the page." He then set down, both in his words and hers, about twenty of the remarks that he remembered she had made — on her family, her reading, and her thoughts about poetry. She conversed, as she wrote, in aphorisms. "Women talk; men are silent. That is why I dread women." "Truth is such a rare thing it is delightful to tell it." "Is it oblivion or absorption when things pass from our minds?" Twenty years later Higginson recalled that there had not been a trace of affectation either in her manner or her words, but he adds that he had found her "much too enigmatical a being for me to solve in an hour's interview, and an instinct told me that the slightest attempt at direct cross-examination would make her withdraw into her shell; I could only sit and watch, as one does in the woods." She seems indeed to have cast her spell.

She wrote him next a month later, and the impression of his visit was still sharp: "After you went I took Macbeth and turned to 'Birnam Wood.' Came twice 'to Dunsinane' — I thought and went about my work. I remember your coming as serious sweetness placed now with the Unreal. . . The vein cannot thank the artery — but her solemn indebtedness to him, even the stolidest admit and so of me who try, whose effort leaves no sound." Had Higginson perhaps talked more than he remembered doing? He had evidently questioned her about some things, though she must have evaded making answers. "You ask great questions accidentally," she goes on. "To answer them would be events. I trust you are safe." The enigmatic joining of the three short sentences in one paragraph may have seemed casual to the observer who had judged her to be "thoroughly ingenuous & simple." The letter closes with a sentence that combines tenseness with exultation in the manner so peculiarly her own: "Abroad is close tonight and I have but to lift my Hands to touch the 'Hights of Abraham.'" The letter itself is as tense as a coiled spring. It is signed "Dickinson." His coming had allowed her to discharge the greatest debt of gratitude she was ever to feel, and her letters to him thereafter are without urgency, though their relative number during the remaining fifteen years of their correspondence greatly multiplies.

She thenceforth sent him poems from time to time, maintaining the solemn fiction that she was his pupil and would write better if he would "but guide Dickinson." His friendly replies kept her abreast of new authors he thought she might like to hear about. In fact his answer to her September letter spoke of the best-selling Western poet Joaquin Miller. Her four-word summation of the Sierra bard is final. Commenting that she does not read Miller because she cannot care for him, she adds: "Transport is not urged."

There is no question that her admiration for Higginson was genuine, but as time passes one senses a stereotype in the enthusiasm she expresses for his writing, which she seems to admire with more loyalty than zeal. Again in Amherst on December 3, 1873, Higginson paid a second and, as it proved, last call. Neither of them appears to have found the occasion important. He made a perfunctory entry in his diary, and her letter to him in the following January strains somewhat to make appropriate small talk. "Of your flitting Coming it is fair to think. Like the Bee's Coupe—vanishing in Music. Would you with the Bee return, what a Firm of Noon." This sober nonsense could cover a variety of moods, but none better than boredom. It was written in reply to a New Year's gift and a note from him thanking her for having received him. "I am glad to remember my visit to Amherst," he had said, "and especially the time spent with you. It seemed to give you some happiness, and I hope it did—certainly I enjoyed being with you. Each time we seem to come together as old & tried friends; and I certainly feel that I have known you long & well, through the beautiful thoughts and words you have sent me. I hope you will not cease to trust me and turn to me; and I will try to speak the truth to you, and with love." His patterns of address are fashioned to her whimsies, and honestly spoken to the simple, ingenuous person he feels he is writing. And there is no doubt that Emily Dickinson understood him fully. A few days after the visit, but before he had written to her, he wrote to his sisters that he has just seen his "eccentric poetess." "She glided in, in white, bearing a *Daphne odora* for me, and said, under her breath, 'How long are you going to stay?' I'm afraid [my wife] Mary's other remark, 'Oh, why do the insane so cling to you?' still holds." Emily Dickinson had dramatized her entrance, and her opening remark was a gambit that Higginson had not expected. She made another one later on that likewise put him off balance, for he records it in the same letter to his sisters: "She says, 'There is always one thing to be grateful for,—that one is one's self and not somebody else.'" Mary Higginson's comment was, he said, that she thought the remark singularly out of place coming, as it did, from Miss Dickinson. Though the lives of Emily Dickinson and Colonel Higginson in any biographical assessment are inescapably linked, one's wish to explain convincingly their mutual good will is exacerbated by the fact that, on the level they met, the nature of his insights and her genius were antipodal.

With the passing years Emily Dickinson sent Higginson notes on special occasions. After her father's death in 1874, she replied to Higginson's letter of condolence with intimate warmth. A year later she immediately notified him of her mother's paralysis, and during the two years following she wrote him with great frequency. Once she tells him how vividly she recalls reading "your first Book." It was perhaps his one novel *Malbone* (1869), a copy of which Higginson had seen on the parlor table at the time of his first visit. "It was Mansions—Nations—Kinsmen—too—to me." The mood of their relationship is expressed in a sentence she wrote in October 1876, after Helen Hunt Jackson had asked to be allowed to publish the poem "Success." Emily Dickinson asked Colonel Higginson to add his disapproval of the idea to her own. "I am sorry to flee so often to my safest friend, but hope he permits me." The Colonel was willing to oblige.

Mary Channing Higginson was gradually failing. Emily Dickinson sent her a copy of "How know it from a Summer's Day," lines written about Indian summer. Mrs. Higginson's note of acknowledgment gave Emily Dickinson the opportunity to write her three or four notes. One such in the spring of 1877 concludes: "Forgive me if I come too much – the time to live is frugal – and good as is a better earth, it will not quite be this." It was shortly followed by another: "I cannot let the grass come without remembering you, and half resent my rapid Feet, when they are not your's." At about this time she had written the two-stanza poem beginning

> Hope is a strange invention –
> A Patent of the Heart –
> In unremitting Action
> Yet never wearing out –

The letter continues, talking about the beauty of the spring. It then attaches the second stanza — the first is sensitively omitted — to the thought: "Bliss without a price, I earned myself of nature –"

> Of whose electric Adjunct
> Not anything is known –
> Though it's unique Momentum
> Inebriate our own.

Mrs. Higginson died in the following September, and Emily Dickinson wrote to her bereaved friend: "Do not try to be saved – but let Redemption find you – as it certainly will – Love is it's own rescue, for we – at our supremest, are but it's trembling Emblems."

After travel abroad Higginson left Newport to take up residence once more in Cambridge, where he remained until his death in 1911. His second marriage in 1879 to Mary Thacher, the birth of their first daughter, the infant's death, and the birth of another daughter in 1881, were all occasions for letters often incorporating or accompanied by poems. On her side the occasions were all losses of loved ones: her mother, Charles Wadsworth, her nephew Gilbert, and in 1884, Judge Otis Lord of Salem.

Her own final illness was upon her when she learned of the unexpected death of Helen Jackson, in August 1885, and the last letters to Colonel Higginson deal largely with her memory of Mrs. Jackson. She was probably aware of the short time remaining when she wrote him, in the spring of 1886: "I think of you with absent Affection, and the Wife and Child I never have seen, Legend and Love in one." During April she confided to her faithful Norcross cousins that she has "twice been very sick, dears, with a little recess of convalescence, then to be more sick." Her father's youngest sister, Elizabeth Dickinson Currier, but seven years older than herself, received one of her last notes. The jocularity of the tone conceals her knowledge of the seriousness of Libbie's own illness, which likewise shortly proved fatal. "Mr Hunt was tinning a Post this Morning, and told us Libbie did'nt feel quite as well as usual, and I hav'nt felt quite as well as usual since the Chestnuts were ripe, though it was'nt the Chestnuts' fault, but the Crocuses are so martial and the Daffodils to the second joint, let us join Hands and recover."

But her final words were sent to Colonel Higginson and to her cousins. Aware that she could not survive the nephritis from which she suffered, she wrote a note to the Colonel, spelled out with difficulty, and composed perhaps a matter of days before her death on May fifteenth. It is without salutation or signature, and seems indeed to have been her farewell. "Deity – does He live now? My friend – does he breathe?" To Loo and Fanny her message was briefer still: "Little Cousins – Called back."

Higginson attended her funeral four days later, and he recorded the circumstances in his diary. "To Amherst to the funeral of that rare and strange creature, Emily Dickinson. The country exquisite, day perfect, and an atmosphere of its own, fine and strange, about the whole house and grounds — a more saintly and elevated 'House of Usher' . . . E. D.'s face a wondrous restoration of youth . . . not a gray hair or wrinkle, and perfect peace on the beautiful brow . . . I read a poem by Emily Brontë. How large a portion of the people who have most interested me have passed away."

Thus concluded one of the most eventful, and at the same time elusive and insubstantial friendships in the annals of American literature.

The third paragraph of the "Letter to a Young Contributor," the article to which Emily Dickinson had responded on that April day in 1862, opens thus: "Nor is there the slightest foundation for the supposed editorial prejudice against new or obscure contributors. On the contrary, every editor is always hungering and thirsting after novelties. To take the lead in bringing forward a new genius is as fascinating a privilege as that of the physician who boasted to Sir Henry Halford of having been the first man to discover the Asiatic cholera and to communicate it to the public." Higginson had received, during the quarter of a century they had corresponded, one hundred poems. Shortly after her death he consented to edit, with Mabel Loomis Todd, the volumes of *Poems* that were published in 1890 and 1891, but he did so reluctantly. Emily Dickinson had learned during the summer of 1862 just how far Higginson was willing to go in taking the lead in bringing forward a new genius. Now, as her editor, he had permanently associated his name with hers. But during the remaining twenty years of his life he never became fully convinced that his decision to publish the poems had been entirely a credit to his critical judgment.

V I

THE BUSINESS OF CIRCUMFERENCE:
Meaning in Poetry

IN HER FOURTH LETTER to Higginson, Emily Dickinson came closer to defining her poetics than she ever did before or after. Her declaration is a sentence of four words. Promising to obey every precept he will give her, though she knew she would never observe any, she adds: "And for this, Preceptor, I shall bring you . . . every gratitude I know." But the fanciful extravagance leads into one of the most serious statements she ever made: "Perhaps you smile at me. I could not stop for that. My Business is Circumference."

The two words that Emily Dickinson returns to again and again are *awe* and *circumference*. At one level she associates them with cosmic expanse and the unknowable, and they must be interpreted in terms of her religious thinking. But they also explain her theory of poetics, and they are linked in meaning. Her intent in creating a poem is to elicit "awe" from the object or idea by which she is inspired, and to project it with "circumference." The terms as she uses them, though they do not lend themselves to exact definition, can be explained in a general way. She felt "awe" when she recognized a poem by the physical sensation of cold or heat. She "sings," she had explained to Higginson, because she is afraid. She writes verses to relieve a "palsy" when her attention is troubled by "a sudden light on Orchards, or a new fashion in the wind." These objects fill her with awe to such a degree that she begs to be allowed to write him, to be his "scholar," to have the protection of his counsel. All sensitive people share her love of hills, the sundown, the noise in the pool. Few feel "awe" to the point where, "if caught with the Dawn, or the Sunset," they would feel themselves to be "the only Kangaroo among the Beauty." The extent to which she was subject to such an emotion she fully recognized as an affliction, and calls it so, hoping that "instruction" from him might relieve it. The condition is not one which she had brought upon herself. "I suppose," she concludes in discussing the problem, that "the pride that stops the Breath, in the Core of Woods, is not of Ourself." The solemn wonder, the profound and reverent dread is a fear, a terror, inspired by deity. This is the Awe that she felt to be never far away, and she wishes to take her tutor's hand when the woods become too dark to penetrate alone.

"No man saw awe" she begins one poem, though it is concealed in the most commonplace experiences. Awe, here personified, has never admitted people to his house, which men have passed often, not recognizing it at first. As soon as recognition comes, they flee. Moses, who looked on God, saw awe. A like sensation equates poetry and love:

> To pile like Thunder to it's close
> Then crumble grand away
> While Everything created hid
> This – would be Poetry –
>
> Or Love – the two coeval come –
> We both and neither prove –
> Experience either and consume –
> For None see God and live –

There is a hint of what she feels in this early quatrain:

> It's such a little thing to weep –
> So short a thing to sigh –
> And yet – by Trades – the size of *These*
> We men and women die!

This is not a sentimental assessment of life as a vale of tears. It is a lightning flash that illuminates the stupendousness of the most ordinary crises of living. Through the experience of our hearts, not our minds, we come alive. "To be alive is power," she exclaimed to Higginson. Mere existence, even "without a further function," is "Omnipotence Enough." She wrote her Norcross cousins in March 1862, having in mind the death of Elizabeth Barrett Browning during the previous summer: "I noticed that Robert Browning had made another poem, and was astonished — till I remembered that I, myself, in my smaller way, sang off charnel steps. Every day life feels mightier, and what we have the power to be, more stupendous." There is a vitality in the way she thought and expressed herself so urgent as to be almost aggressive. It must have extended likewise to her daily associations, and one can easily understand why she had to learn to shield herself by retreat from personal contacts. When Higginson asked her on the occasion of his first call whether the circumscription of her life did not leave her with a feeling of want, she replied that she could not conceive of such in all future time. Then she paused and added: "I feel that I have not expressed myself strongly enough."

Her private association with place names is tied closely into the way she projected her imagination. Cashmere and the Indies typify opulence. But most such names are not used to suggest escape into romance. Calvary, linked with Wadsworth, like Gethsemane is associated with agony. Ophir, Potosi, Teneriffe, the Himmaleh represent distance, wealth, limitless vista, unassailable height, and all are awesome prospects. One lives in a world where the passage of ants across the kitchen floor opens like vistas, and to pursue lines of thought which they may suggest will lead one to astounding discoveries. One such privately used word is "Etruscan," and she evidently felt it to be associated with an untranslatable language, or with a great civilization, itself unknown, transmitted to breed other important but unforeseeable ways of living. "Please consult the bees – they are the only authority on Etruscan matters." She addressed a note to accompany a wedding gift to the girl "who is about to make the Etruscan Experiment." In the poem "Unto like Story," that which beckons toward light is the "Etruscan invitation."

Even the emotion of embarrassment can be akin to awe, because sometimes it is linked with our recognition that in each of us is a depth that can never really be sounded by another.

> Embarrassment of one another
> And God
> Is Revelation's limit,
> Aloud
> Is nothing that is chief,
> But still,
> Divinity dwells under seal.

The portentousness with which she regarded the future she expressed thus:

> The Future – never spoke –
> Nor will He – like the Dumb –
> Reveal by sign – a syllable
> Of His Profound To Come –
>
> But when the News be ripe –
> Presents it – in the Act –
> Forestalling Preparation –
> Escape – or Substitute –
>
> Indifferent to Him –
> The Dower – as the Doom –
> His Office – but to execute
> Fate's – Telegram – to Him –

The Short Meter conveys her thought with the urgency which the word "Telegram" is intended to suggest. The irregular rhyme of the second stanza and the suspended rhyme of the third carry forward the mood of indifference which fate itself is depicted as showing. The inexorableness is thus made awesome.

On two or three occasions she tried to manufacture a sense of terror and dismay. Her talents did not lie in that direction, and such contrived poems as "I know some lonely Houses off the Road," and "I Years had been from Home" seem pallid rather than spectral. It is when she writes about the wonder and terror inherent in one's own existence that she casts her spell.

> One need not be a Chamber – to be Haunted –
> One need not be a House –
> The Brain has Corridors – surpassing
> Material Place –
>
> Far safer, of a Midnight Meeting
> External Ghost
> Than it's interior Confronting –
> That Cooler Host.
>
> Far safer, through an Abbey gallop,
> The Stones a'chase –
> Than Unarmed, one's a'self encounter –
> In lonesome Place –
>
> Ourself behind ourself, concealed –
> Should startle most –
> Assassin hid in our Apartment
> Be Horror's least.
>
> The Body – borrows a Revolver –
> He bolts the Door –
> O'erlooking a superior spectre –
> Or More –

One of the fully realized poems dealing with the theme of awe is haunting as very few poems ever become. It seems to touch upon her acceptance of her destiny, not only as a poet but as a particular kind of poet. Her assurance of this fate did not come early in her life, and by the time she had made her adjustment to it, in 1863 when this poem was evidently written, she could look with some objectivity both forward and backward. The concrete imagery is in the great ballad tradition. The idea of the first stanza is as startling as the figure of speech itself. She has always stood a loaded gun, but the owner, the animating spirit within that creates or withholds creation at will, identified her as his possession somewhat belatedly. Since he made his identification and claim, she as a physical entity has served her master with consecrated devotion.

> My Life had stood – a Loaded Gun –
> In Corners – till a Day
> The Owner passed – identified –
> And carried Me away –
>
> And now We roam in Sovreign Woods –
> And now We hunt the Doe –
> And every time I speak for Him –
> The Mountains straight reply –
>
> And do I smile, such cordial light
> Upon the Valley glow –
> It is as a Vesuvian face
> Had let it's pleasure through –
>
> And when at Night – Our good Day done –
> I guard My Master's Head –
> 'Tis better than the Eider – Duck's
> Deep Pillow – to have shared –
>
> To foe of His – I'm deadly foe –
> None stir the second time –
> On whom I lay a Yellow Eye –
> Or an emphatic Thumb –
>
> Though I than He – may longer live
> He longer must – than I –
> For I have but the power to kill,
> Without – the power to die –

She concludes that she, the body that guards the animating spirit, may outlive her inspiration, but she hopes that nothing so dire will happen. For the body is function only, as the function of a gun is to kill. Condemned to live without inspiration would be more terrifying than death, which one is powerless to summon at will. The association of inspiration with a loaded gun, controlled by an inner identity, becomes more startling when it is placed beside a sentence that she used in a letter written about this time to Higginson. "I had no Monarch in my life, and cannot rule myself, and when I try to organize – my little Force explodes – and leaves me bare and charred."

The Circumference that Emily Dickinson wishes to make her business is somewhat difficult to explain because she intends to remove it from the context of logic. "You'll know it," she begins one poem — referring apparently to the recognition of some ultimate truth — "as you know 'tis Noon – By Glory"; and asserts

> By intuition, Mightiest Things
> Assert themselves – and not by terms.

She once wrote a friend: "The Bible dealt with the Centre, not with Circumference." In context, she means that the Bible laid down precepts or it prophesied or was insistent upon particular values. As nearly as one can judge from the nature of her thinking and the pattern of her poems, the term "circumference" meant a projection of her imagination into all relationships of man, nature, and spirit.

> When Bells stop ringing – Church – begins –
> The Positive – of Bells –
> When Cogs – stop – that's Circumference –
> The Ultimate – of Wheels.

As a possible alternative reading for "Positive" she suggests "Transitive." Logically stated as prose, this quatrain of nineteen words expresses the thought that the reality of experience is not found in sensation. It is in the translation of the sensation into its positive or transitive meaning. Only by pausing in the daily round of meshing one cog into another can we discover meaning. Ultimate meaning, the whole, like a circle, projects itself back upon itself. A similar meaning for the word is in the poem dealing with Judgment Day. At that time there will be a gathering so vast that "No Crowd that has occurred" can equal it. This is the moment when "Circumference be full," for nothing can duplicate or parallel the significance of the occasion "To Universe – and Me."

In one poem written late in her life she calls circumference the bride of awe. In April 1884 Daniel Chester French's statue of John Harvard was unveiled in front of University Hall in Cambridge. Emily Dickinson had known French as a boy in Amherst when his father, Henry Flagg French, served briefly as the first president of Massachusetts Agricultural College from 1864 to 1866. After reading of the unveiling, she wrote the young sculptor a letter of congratulation, concluding: "Success is dust, but an aim forever touched with dew. God keep you fundamental." She then added this quatrain:

> Circumference thou Bride of Awe
> Possessing thou shalt be
> Possessed by every hallowed Knight
> That dares to covet thee

The artist is that person who, by giving transitive meaning to sensation, can inspire solemn wonder or amazement in the beholder.

Emily Dickinson felt both "a nearness to tremendousness," as one poem phrases it, and an awe of the familiar. She intends to make it her business to give them poetic form. Mystical experience of course cannot be defined. It is to her credit as an artist that she did not try to define one experience in terms of another. Her clear vision of things as they are would not allow her to indulge in the romantic vagueness of seeing God either in a buttercup or a volcanic eruption. "Circumference" is a way, the way that she chose, of projecting herself into phenomena and describing each as it abides or inheres alone. "A Coffin – is a small Domain" she says, yet it is ampler than the sun, and to the one who there bestows a friend it is

> Circumference without Relief –
> Or Estimate – or End –

Here the word suggests unimaginable spacial distances. Her artistic credo she made explicit in 1876 when, in an aphoristic mood she wrote Higginson the single sentence: "Nature is a Haunted House but Art – a House that tries to be haunted." The world of nature is a house in which we live, and it is haunted, as all must feel who pause to observe. It is the function of the artist to create awe, to "haunt" the reader or beholder by the created imitation. Houses are always awesome when they are empty and we explore them alone. Though the aphorism was written late, the image of exploration and the same figure of art as a "house" she had envisioned as early as 1862.

> I dwell in Possibility –
> A fairer House than Prose –
> More numerous of Windows –
> Superior – for Doors –
>
> Of Chambers as the Cedars –
> Impregnable of Eye –
> And for an Everlasting Roof
> The Gambrels of the Sky –
>
> Of Visitors – the fairest –
> For Occupation – This –
> The spreading wide my narrow Hands
> To gather Paradise –

The house is provided for all, for it is the world of nature, the fairest residence imaginable, where one may gather paradise, like grapes or apples, by merely spreading wide one's hands. Her function, and by extension the function of any artist, is to take advantage of this excellent structure, admitting as it does so much airiness and light. The artist needs only to make it express her personality in such a way that visitors will be enchanted. The possibilities of the unimproved are limitless and exhilarating. Hers was a particularly domestic world. But the love of an artfully appointed home, or created poem, is universal.

Emily Dickinson's aesthetic credo is most substantially revealed in her concept of beauty, and the philosophy of all her Puritan past is transmuted into art in her poems on the nature of beauty. Like salvation, it comes as a grace, an infusion from without, an emanation which the creature passively receives and is powerless to win by effort to attain it. It is not merely similar to God's love, but is in fact God's love for man. It is the love which possesses those who are willing to pass through the straight pass of suffering to discover the redemption which offers immortality.

> I died for Beauty – but was scarce
> Adjusted in the Tomb
> When One who died for Truth, was lain
> In an adjoining Room –
>
> He questioned softly "Why I failed"?
> "For Beauty," I replied –
> "And I – for Truth – Themself are One –
> We Brethren, are," He said –
>
> And so, as Kinsmen, met a Night –
> We talked between the Rooms –
> Until the Moss had reached our lips –
> And covered up – our names –

Beauty inheres, it cannot be fashioned or formed. "Beauty – be not caused – It Is." An ecstatic experience, like heaven, cannot be defined.

> The Definition of Beauty is
> That Definition is none –
> Of Heaven, easing Analysis,
> Since Heaven and He are One.

Yet the beholder or listener must be willing to possess:

> To hear an Oriole sing
> May be a common thing –
> Or only a divine.
>
> It is not of the Bird
> Who sings the same, unheard,
> As unto Crowd –
>
> The Fashion of the Ear
> Attireth that it hear
> In Dun, or fair –

So whether it be Rune,
Or whether it be none
Is of within.

The "Tune is in the Tree –"
The Skeptic – showeth me –
"No Sir! In Thee!"

She is not thinking of death, but of the encroachment of the super-nal, when she exclaims:

Beauty crowds me till I die
Beauty, mercy have on me
But if I expire today
Let it be in sight of thee –

The experience of beauty is a moral quality, won through redemptive suffering:

Must be a Wo –
A loss or so –
To bend the eye
Best Beauty's way –

But – once aslant
It notes Delight
As difficult
As Stalactite –

A Common Bliss
Were had for less –
The price – is
Even as the Grace –

Our lord – thought no
Extravagance
To pay – a Cross –

The bliss won easily is not beauty. Though the word as she uses it connotes the sensations received by observing the natural order in the world about us, she is talking about its redemptive quality. The discernment of beauty is an intellectual experience, in the sense that it can be perceived only by those who in fact take on the image of God. "Is it Intellect that the Patriot means when he speaks of his 'Native Land'?" she wrote Higginson. In the beginning was the word, she is always aware, and the magic of language constantly elates her.

> Strong Draughts of Their Refreshing Minds
> To drink – enables Mine
> Through Desert or the Wilderness
> As bore it Sealed Wine –
>
> To go elastic – Or as One
> The Camel's trait – attained –
> How powerful the Stimulus
> Of an Hermetic Mind –

The poet, by consenting to the preordained suffering whereby creation is achieved, gains status, and the language he utters, being of God, bestows immortality. Such a concept is by no means original with Emily Dickinson, who knew her Shakespeare intimately.

> Essential Oils – are wrung –
> The Attar from the Rose
> Be not expressed by Suns – alone –
> It is the gift of Screws –
>
> The General Rose – decay –
> But this – in Lady's Drawer
> Make Summer – When the Lady lie
> In Ceaseless Rosemary –

Most of the poems that equate beauty with immortality were written in 1862 and 1863. That which is beautiful is experienced both by the heart and the mind. We cannot comprehend its immensity nor be estranged from it. Our destiny is involved in it. What Emily Dickinson knew about Jonathan Edwards came to her by way of the Valley tradition, which stressed his sterner doctrines. She would probably have been surprised to know that the quatrain she wrote in the late seventies is a twenty-word summary of Edwards' thoughts on the subject, expressed one hundred and twenty years before in his greatest essay, *The Nature of True Virtue.*

> Estranged from Beauty – none can be –
> For Beauty is Infinity –
> And power to be finite ceased
> Before Identity was leased –

On the artist is bestowed the gift that invests him with enduring rank.

> The One who could repeat the Summer day
> Were greater than itself – though He
> Minutest of Mankind should be –
>
> And He – could reproduce the Sun –
> At period of going down –
> The Lingering – and the Stain – I mean –
>
> When Orient have been outgrown –
> And Occident – become Unknown –
> His Name – remain –

Among artists she best understood poets, and had intimate knowledge of the poetic process. It is coeval with love, she knows, but it cannot be explained: "For None see God and live." Her own dedication to poetry she expressed in 1862, the year that she wrote most of her verses on the function and status of the poet. "The Soul selects her own Society – Then – shuts the Door." The poet is blessed, but isolated. Her letter to the world from which she is shut away will transmit such news about nature as she has received through her senses.

> This is my letter to the World
> That never wrote to Me –
> The simple News that Nature told –
> With tender Majesty

Her Message is committed
To Hands I cannot see –
For love of Her – Sweet – countrymen –
Judge tenderly – of Me

It is expected of the poet that he will distill amazing sense from ordinary meanings, extract attar from the familiar, which otherwise would perish. Such is the theme of "This was a Poet," with its conclusion that:

Of Pictures, the Discloser –
The Poet – it is He –
Enables Us – by Contrast –
To ceaseless Poverty.

Of Portion – so unconscious –
The Robbing – could not harm –
Himself – to Him – a Fortune –
Exterior – to Time –

To be a poet is:

A privilege so awful
What would the Dower be,
Had I the Art to stun myself
With Bolts of Melody!

She is concerned with craftsmanship in "Myself was formed – a Carpenter," and with the destiny of the poet in "The Martyr Poets did not tell," and "I reckon – when I count at all – / First – Poets." But her final words on the subject she spoke in 1864. They exemplify as art the concept of fame that she had expressed to Higginson two years earlier – that if it belonged to her she could not escape it. Circumference is her business.

The Poets light but Lamps –
Themselves – go out –
The Wicks they stimulate –
If vital Light

Inhere as do the Suns –
Each Age a Lens
Disseminating their
Circumference –

It is of primary importance to bear in mind that when Emily
Dickinson wrote her first letter to Higginson, asking him to pass
judgment upon the poems she enclosed, her aesthetic theory was
fully established. Though she protested in every letter which she
wrote during the ensuing months that she was grateful for his
"surgery," that she needed his frank criticism and would obediently
follow his precepts, the fact is that she never at any time conformed
to his injunctions. The prescriptions that he wrote out were intended for a beginner who, he implied, had a great deal to learn
before she could qualify as a poet worthy of public attention.

Clearly Emily Dickinson had no formal theory of poetics, in the
sense that she could have written a critique in the manner of Poe.
But she had a developed and consistent idea of the manner in
which the poet is inspired. Her ideas are conventional to the degree
that they are in the main stream from Plato to Emerson. The poet
is a seer; his inspiration comes as a grace, overleaping regular chan-
nels; he is thus a man possessed, who reveals truth out of the agony
of his travail; and the anguish of such possession enables the re-
ceiver to partake of reality and reveal at least a fragment of the
mysteries that the heart perceives. Such possession cannot be made
comprehensible to others by instruction. Uncontrolled, it leads into
the sheer nonsense of automatic writing. She had no more success
than any other artist has ever had in giving form to every creative
impulse. But her successes, she seems to have felt by 1862, were
increasingly evident. She persistently labored to file her lines so
that the images would be exact and sharp. She was aware that form
is inherent in the created object, and she achieved control when
her perceptions gave shape to the object before her pen touched
paper. The abandoned worksheet drafts are examples of imperfectly
wrought images; that is, of language uncontrolled by an inherent

form. Her successful poems were those in which both elements coalesce. Her failures, almost without exception, are the poems in which the form was not first inherent. An excellent example of such a failure is her poem about two butterflies. Her intent seems to have been to make their lightness and parting motion inhere. This she wrote in 1862:

Two Butterflies went out at Noon –
And waltzed upon a Farm –
Then stepped straight through the Firmament
And rested, on a Beam –

And then – together bore away
Upon a shining Sea –
Though never yet, in any Port –
Their coming, mentioned – be–

If spoken by the distant Bird –
If met in Ether Sea
By Frigate, or by Merchantman –
No notice – was – to me –

By the time she reaches the end, her focus is so blurred that the reader has forgotten what she was writing about. She was aware of failure, and many years later began all over again. But inspiration was not with her. This penciled worksheet draft survives, and is rare in the degree of its complication. She never completed the poem, which remains a fascinating document of poetic creativeness in travail:

[stanza 1]

Two Butterflies went out at Noon
And waltzed upon a Farm
And then espied Circumference
Then overtook –
And caught a ride with him –
    and took a Bout with him –

DWELLER IN POSSIBILITY

[stanza 2]

Then lost themselves and found themselves
    staked   lost
    chased   caught
In eddies of the sun –
    Fathoms in
    Rapids of
    Gambols with
        of
For Frenzy zies of
    antics in
      with
Till Rapture *missed them*
        missed her footing –
          Peninsula
  Gravitation chased
      humbled –
      ejected
      foundered
      grumbled
Until a Zephyr pushed them
      chased –
      flung –
      spurned
      scourged
And Both were wrecked in Noon –
      drowned –
      quenched –
      whelmed –
And they were hurled from noon –

[stanza 3]

To all surviving Butterflies
Be this Fatuity
    Biography –
Example – and monition
To entomology –

150

Emily Dickinson commented to Higginson: "If I read a book and it makes my whole body so cold no fire ever can warm me, I know *that* is poetry. If I feel physically as if the top of my head were taken off, I know *that* is poetry. These are the only ways I know it. Is there any other way?" There are to be sure other ways that poetry may be known, but there was no other way that she could successfully write it. Her instinct led her to employ her talents correctly. One hardly thinks of such masterpieces as *Lycidas* or *Alexander's Feast* as the performance of men who felt that the top of their heads was being taken off. Yet the end in view for Dickinson, as it had been for Milton and Dryden, was the creation of a work of art wherein the form was inherently part of the idea.

The immediate sources of Emily Dickinson's inspiration sprang from the associations she most deeply cherished and about which she felt greatest awe. First was the world about her, the moods of nature, the creatures of earth and air that scamper and soar, and the buds that bloom and fade. Equally important were friends, always held in a brittle remembrance by her acute consciousness that death at any moment can occur. And lurking behind every thought to which she gave expression was the abiding wonder, the craving for assurance, about the sempiternal. Her relation to nature, death, and immortality she made the "flood subject" of all she wrote. How did she clothe the ideas? What was the metaphor of her thinking?

Basically the words and phrases by which she makes one idea denote likeness to another are cast from the images which she absorbed from the Bible. It was the primary source, and no other is of comparable importance. Even when she draws her figures of speech from the language of the sea, of trade, of law, or of science, they usually suggest that they have passed through the alembic of the King James version of biblical utterance.

> The Sweets of Pillage, can be known
> To no one but the Thief –
> Compassion for Integrity
> Is his divinest Grief –

The theme of compassionate love draws for its metaphor upon the most famous incident of such love. At the moment of Christ's supreme trial, He extends mercy to the repentant thief. There are several score of poems where the biblical metaphor is direct and self-evident. But the shaping of her thought in terms of biblical incident, events, and precept is apparent in almost every poem that she wrote. She transmuted universals into particulars by means of such figures of speech: "location's narrow way," "the smitten rock," "broad possessions," "this accepted breath," "the scarlet way," "the morning stars," "the straight pass of suffering," "the apple on the tree," "the sapphire fellows," "moat of pearl," "the fleshy gate," "this meek apparelled thing," "the primer to a life." All are drawn from the Bible, and require on the part of the reader a like familiarity if the full import is to be rendered. Let two examples suffice. The first stanza of a poem in which she imagines herself dead, and speculates on how the living might show their grief, goes thus:

> 'Twas just this time, last year I died,
> I know I heard the Corn,
> When I was carried by the Farms —
> It had the Tassels on —

The year is at its full. Apples are ready for garnering, "And Carts went stooping round the fields/ To take the Pumpkins in." The expression "I heard the Corn" does not mean that in her mind's ear she hears it growing. The line echoes Hosea 2.22, wherein the corn (and wine and oil) cry to be harvested. It is typical of her method to combine a metaphor drawn from a universal cultural heritage with objects familiar to her daily experience: carts, pumpkins, and cornfields.

She drew from about thirty books of the Bible. The three books that echo most persistently in her poems and letters are Matthew, Revelation, and Genesis — in that order. They are followed closely by John, I and II Corinthians, Exodus, and Psalms. She breathed the atmosphere of biblical lore, and inevitably the figures with which she clothed her ideas are permeated with it. The rhyme and metric pattern of "Just lost, when I was saved!" have already been analyzed,* but the extent to which it depends upon the Bible for its imagery may not at first be apparent. Several words in the first stanza have biblical association in a general way, including *lost, saved, girt, Eternity, breath.* The imagery in the remaining three stanzas derives from Revelation, chapters 1, 4, and 5, and from I Corinthians. The pale reporter is John at Patmos who fell as dead at Christ's feet. The beginning of John's vision occurs before the door that opened into heaven. God's purpose and promise is set forth in the book sealed to human knowledge. It is in Corinthians that the idea is made explicit concerning the limits of human wisdom: "Eye hath not seen, nor ear heard . . . the things which God hath prepared for them that love him." The poem, written about 1860, may be her first to give immediacy to the theme that she never ceased to ponder: our nearness to ultimate reality would lead us to believe that we could surely discover it by determined effort, yet we must accept the inevitable, realizing that we cannot win through to an understanding of it during our mortal years.

It is not too much to say that in almost every poem she wrote, there are echoes of her sensitivity to the idiom of the Bible, and of her dependence upon its imagery for her own striking figures of speech. The great reservoir of classical myth she rarely drew upon. Since she never uses figures of speech for embellishment, she preferred those which for her had the power to evoke deep emotion. She found the Bible her key to meaning, and shaped her words and symbols by way of the stories and precepts in its reduceless mines.

On that portentous April day when Emily Dickinson first wrote Higginson, her question was: "Will an accredited literary judge believe that I am an authentic poet?" The question had its practical side, for assembled about her was a teeming body of verse, and somehow a way of sharing it must be found. There were in fact three more years of full creativeness. In 1863 she wrote some one hundred and fifty poems; in 1864, well over a hundred; and about

* See pages 89–90.

seventy or so in 1865. After that, throughout her life, the yearly average never exceeded twenty, one half of which never progressed beyond the worksheet stage. Several of the later poems are imperishable lyrics, but she would never again be driven by the frenzy that possessed her in the early sixties. She achieved an intensity, passionate and despairing at first, then restrained, that gives to her poetry of those years the quality of "circumference" and "awe" that she intended.

VII

HELEN OF COLORADO: Achievement

AFTER HER EARLY AND UNEXPECTED DEATH at fifty-four, the qualities remarked on by those who remembered Helen Hunt Jackson best were her candor and bright impetuosity, her charm of manner and conversation, and her feminine sense of style in dress. These characteristics, still evident in her letters and photographs, suggest a vivid, gifted personality. She swung into the ken of Emily Dickinson in the last decade of their lives, but her impact led the unknown poet to the same extravagant praise that Helen Jackson won from other contemporaries. In language that draws upon Browning's "The Last Ride Together" for its hyperbole, Emily expressed herself afterwards: "I never saw Mrs Jackson but twice, but those twice were indelible – and one day more – I am deified – was the only impression she ever left on any heart (house) she entered." And again at the same time she said: "Helen of Troy will die, but Helen of Colorado, never."

In spite of the fact that Helen Jackson came very late into Emily Dickinson's life and had no influence whatsoever upon her writing, to the greater poet the lesser poet's accomplishments seemed dazzling. And why not? "What is this world? what asketh men to have?" once asked Chaucer's dying Arcite. One woman chose to dwell in obscurity. The other invited the public notice which brought her a substantial acclaim in her lifetime. Any link in the history of such careers is important, quite beyond the interest one may have in the individual biographies, because the careers themselves shed light on the way writers live. Each came to respect the other's choice. Each realized that neither could have altered her destiny. But both left expressions to the effect that the other's way of life was incomprehensible.

There are circumstances in the lives of Emily Dickinson and Helen Jackson that are curiously parallel. Both were born late in 1830 in Amherst, children of eminent members of the college family. Devoted to literature, both shared an aversion to publicity, one by resisting solicitation that she publish, the other by escaping into a variety of pseudonyms of which "H. H." was the least veiling. Both were gifted personalities, remembered by their friends as brilliant individualists. Their life span was nearly the same. Helen Jackson died nine months before Emily Dickinson, in August 1885. But the differences in their careers are even more striking.

One never married, and remained a lifelong resident of her Amherst homestead, scarcely moving beyond the limit of her gardens, as a way of intensifying her perceptions. The other, twice wed, moved restlessly from Europe to California, and filled her later years by zealous service to philanthropic causes. One kept to the circle of her friends; the other was a publicist who believed that the gifted should sing aloud. One, unknown at her death, is a world poet; the other, lavishly applauded in her day, has settled into history.

Such a comparison does not disparage Helen Jackson. She commanded an eloquence when she wrote her indictment of the white man's treatment of the Indian in *Ramona* that still moves the reader. And she had insights about the poetry of Emily Dickinson that were more penetrating than those of any other qualified judge who, during Dickinson's lifetime, evaluated her poetry. It is Helen Jackson's fate today that the volumes of poems and stories which flooded from her pen and seemed so timeless to her contemporaries now gather dust, and that her memory lives chiefly by the reflected light of the Amherst friend whose reticences she deplored.

Helen Fiske was a daughter of Nathan Welby Fiske, professor of moral philosophy and metaphysics, and Deborah Vinal Fiske. When Helen was four years old, the Fiskes moved to a house on

Pleasant Street within easy walking distance of the Dickinson house on Main Street, and on one occasion about that time the two girls played together "beneath the syringas." For a brief time they attended the same elementary school, and then saw no more of each other for a very great many years.

From the age of ten Helen went to school in various towns nearby. Mrs. Fiske was dying of consumption and the task of caring for her two daughters, Helen and Helen's younger sister Ann, was beyond her strength. Helen was thirteen at the time of her mother's death, and three years later, in 1847, the children were orphaned by the death of their father. In the care of an aunt living in Falmouth, Helen continued her desultory education at Ipswich Female Academy, and concluded it about 1850 at Abbott's Institute in New York City. In October 1852 she married Lieutenant (later Major) Edward Bissell Hunt, an army engineer. Their first son Murray lived eleven months. In 1863 Major Hunt, while conducting an experiment in line of duty, was accidentally killed. Another son Warren, known as Rennie, survived his father by two years, but was fatally stricken at the age of nine.

This utter bereavement completely altered the direction of Helen Hunt's life. Until her husband's death her time had been absorbed by her family and the social demands of army life. After the death of Rennie in April 1865 she had need to call upon all the inner resources she could command. She began writing poetry, and in July the *Nation* published her first poem. Other poems appeared there during the summer, and in Godwin's *New York Evening Post*. By October she felt secure enough about her newly discovered talent to write Godwin to ask his frank opinion whether he believed she was capable of making a profession of her writing. He encouraged her to do so, and commissioned her to write some "pleasant and gossipy" letters on life in Boston. Her career as author was launched. Early in 1866 she went to Newport, Rhode Island, and took rooms at Mrs. Dame's, the boarding house in which Colonel Higginson and his wife resided. In view of the fact that she believed Higginson to be the finest literary craftsman of the day and very shortly had made him promise to act as her literary executor, one suspects that her choice of Newport and Mrs. Dame's was part of a plan to advance her own skills by becoming his protégé. Higginson remarks in his *Journal* that he found the new arrival, this widow in deep mourning, to be a charming and clever addition. His brand of literary affability was especially congenial to her talents, and during the year she began to contribute the articles and book reviews to the New York *Independent*; over the years they numbered some four hundred. She rapidly mastered her craft under Higginson's tutelage, and within two years of the time she began writing, Higginson was able to add her name to his roster of the leading female poets in America. She returned the compliment by a close study of his prose style. She set herself the exercise of trying to alter his paragraphs by deletion or addition, or by changes in wording, in an effort at improvement, but conceded the perfection of his style by confessing herself indeed unable to better it.

Helen Hunt was endowed by nature with the aptitudes that Higginson admired. She wrote with elegance and feeling. Her independence of thought gave zest to her opinions. The decorous ideality in the relationships of her characters did not strike him, or her reading public either, as improbable or vaguely unwholesome. She had learned how to supply readers of popular journals with what they liked. Thus the editors of the journals named, and shortly the editors of other magazines such as *Hearth and Home* and *Scribner's Monthly*, found her writing very marketable. Higginson never erred in spotting talent, but his faculties extended no further. His limitations, greater than Helen Hunt's, did her no harm at least. Higginson found himself in the congenial position of being asked for literary guidance by two women writers, contemporaries who once, briefly in childhood, had gone to school together. Indeed, Helen Hunt made him a confidant during the sixties to the extent that he pledged himself to burn all her letters in the event of her death. He wrote Mrs. Todd many years later that he believed most of the letters that "H. H." had written were probably destroyed: ". . . and not without reason, for she lived in the moment & was a most hazardous correspondent." Sometimes, as he knew, her candor became embarrassingly frank.

During the mid-sixties Higginson told Helen Hunt what he knew about Emily Dickinson, perhaps with the idea of bringing them together. " 'H. H.' did not know of her poems," he told Mrs. Todd, "till I showed them to her (about 1866), and was very little in Amherst after that. But she remembered her at school." Neither of the women made any attempt at the time to renew an association so dim as to be meaningless. Among the scraps of Dickinson papers is an envelope addressed about 1866 in Dickinson's hand to Mrs. Helen Hunt, who visited Amherst during that summer. The evidence tantalizes conjecture but establishes with certainty only that some line of communication was being attempted. Mrs. Hunt was in Amherst again in 1870, but in that year there is no record even of an attempt to meet.

Higginson recorded in the memorandum he made after his call on Emily Dickinson in 1870: "Major Hunt interested her more than any man she ever saw. She remembered two things he said — that her great dog 'understood gravitation' & when he said he should come again 'in a year. If I say a shorter time it will be longer.' " In 1860 both Hunts were in Amherst for the month of August. Helen Hunt wrote to her sister that she and her husband attended church with the Dickinson family and expected to call on the Dickinsons in the evening. That may well have been the occasion when Hunt encountered Emily's dog Carlo. Hunt is reported to have said that he thought Emily herself uncanny. Thus she and the Hunts did casually meet many years before her friendship with Mrs. Hunt ripened. He made some remarks that amused Emily Dickinson, who continued to think him interesting, and he then passed out of her life, as well as his own, thinking her most odd.

In 1871 the first of the *Saxe Holm's Stories* began to appear in *Scribner's Monthly*. They were published anonymously, and Mrs. Hunt never acknowledged that she wrote them. The last of the six in series one, "Esther Wynn's Love-Letters," closely parallels in plot certain features of Emily Dickinson's life, and some biographers have speculated that the two must have worked in collaboration. The story concerns poems and letters, found in a box hidden for fifty years, written by a highly talented but unknown woman to a man whom she could not marry. Mrs. Hunt had seen the poems that Emily Dickinson had sent to Colonel Higginson from time to time, and had learned from him presumably as much as he could tell her. She certainly knew the various brands of Amherst gossip. She therefore had a made-to-order plot for her *Scribner's* readers, with the protection of an anonymity that she never surrendered. The letters and the poems created in the course of the story are sentimental imitations of Emily Dickinson's, verging on unintentional parody; obviously Mrs. Hunt was drawing upon her imagination.

In 1872 Helen Hunt came from California to summer in the White Mountains, and among the Dickinson scraps is another envelope in Emily's hand, addressed to Mrs. Hunt at Bethlehem. One speculates just why these scraps survive. Obviously they were never sent. Perhaps the intended communications were forwarded in substitute envelopes. Perhaps they were addressed pending a decision whether to write a letter, and kept as reminders to herself that she had been thinking of writing. In any event they make clear that some association, however tentative, had been established.

In the summer of 1873 Helen Hunt was vacationing in Princeton, Massachusetts, and wrote Emily Dickinson to inquire about living quarters in Amherst. A reply recommended a comfortable boardinghouse, but before Mrs. Hunt had had time to settle into the rooms, a recurrent bronchial ailment prompted her doctor to hustle her back to Princeton and to accompany her as soon as possible to Colorado Springs. Here she regained her health and met William Sharpless Jackson, a banker and railroad promoter, whom she married two years later in Wolfeboro, New Hampshire, on 22 October 1875.

The earliest surviving letter exchange is a note written to congratulate Mrs. Jackson on her marriage.

Have I a word but joy?
                E. Dickinson
Who fleeing from the Spring
The Spring avenging fling
To Dooms of Balm –

The greeting was warmhearted, but Mrs. Jackson found it perplexing. It was in fact shocking. Who is fleeing? Certainly not Mrs. Jackson. Does "Dooms of Balm" mean a destiny of happiness or a fate requiring sedatives? Mrs. Jackson did not know that Emily Dickinson's keen desire to share the happiness of others was coupled with acute anxiety lest it trespass on privacies. Old friends like the Bowleses and Hollands had long since known how this conflict sometimes resolved itself by a headlong flight from the presence of those she loved best, behavior, distressing to her family, that left Emily abjectly contrite. This impulsive message is headlong but Mrs. Jackson found it intriguing. In her forthright way she wrote back to ask what the lines meant. She even returned the message itself, with this penciled notation on the back: "This is *mine*, remember. You must send it back to me, or else you will be a robber."

The lines had been removed from their original context, but even if Mrs. Jackson had known the whole poem she would still have been mystified.

> Upon a Lilac Sea
> To toss incessantly
> His Plush Alarm
> Who fleeing from the Spring
> The Spring avenging fling
> To Dooms of Balm –

There can be no doubt that what Emily Dickinson meant to convey was her own joy in Mrs. Jackson's new found happiness which she hoped was destined to last. To have the letter returned for an explanation and be compelled to face the truth of her blunder was painful in a way that Mrs. Jackson could never remotely have suspected.

The note thus returned to the sender remains among the Dickinson papers, but not the letter which Mrs. Jackson sent it back in, nor a reply written by Emily Dickinson sometime before the spring of 1876. From Helen Jackson's letter below, written from Colorado Springs on March 20, 1876, one learns that Emily Dickinson's reply included statements to the effect that she would return it and that she had not been annoyed by a request for interpretations. One suspects that in truth she wished Mrs. Jackson would forget the whole wretched affair, and kept the note to help efface all memory of it.

But you did not send it back, though you wrote that you would. Was this an accident, or a late withdrawal of your consent? Remember that it is mine — not yours — and be honest. Thank you for not being angry with my impudent request for interpretations. I do wish I knew just what "dooms" you meant, though! . . .

I hope some day, some where I shall find you in a spot where we can know each other. I wish very much that you would write to me now and then, when it did not bore you. I have a little manuscript volume with a few of your verses in it — and I read them very often — You are a great poet — and it is a wrong to the day you live in, that you will not sing aloud. When you are what men call dead, you will be sorry you were so stingy.

And she signs herself "Yours truly Helen Jackson." The letter establishes the fact that in the spring of 1876 the two women scarcely knew each other; that Mrs. Jackson, by now something of a celebrity, was seeking to initiate a closer relationship; and that she not only had copies of a few Dickinson poems, but also felt convinced of the high rank Emily Dickinson took as a poet. From such a source, this opinion must have been flattering. Its forthrightness is characteristic of "H. H.," and it is a judgment uttered with a conviction which Higginson never came to feel.

Mrs. Jackson knew nothing about Emily Dickinson's earlier experiences with editors. Mrs. Todd states in her journal on the authority of Higginson, who learned it from President Seelye of Amherst, that Emily Dickinson expressed "intense surprise" to Helen Jackson that Helen Jackson could consent to publish: "How can you print a piece of your soul?" Seelye was quoting to Higginson what Mrs. Jackson had told him. One believes the remark was made, but it is open to more interpretations than one. The complexities of publication, as Emily Dickinson had found them, she did not understand, and the vehemence of her comment reflects her bewilderment.

Helen Jackson's earlier letters to Emily Dickinson leave no doubt that Mrs. Jackson knew very little personally about Emily Dickinson's poetry or had ever received any from her. The "manuscript volume" to which she refers must have been a commonplace book into which she transcribed poems that she fancied. Those by Emily Dickinson in all probability derived from copies she had made of some that Colonel Higginson had shown her, and the knowledge of those poems was the impulse that encouraged her now to solicit a correspondence.

The first significant meeting of the two women took place on 10 October 1876, and came about through Helen Jackson's determined insistence. She had come East that summer to oversee the publication of her novel *Mercy Philbrick's Choice,* scheduled for September release. It had been selected as the first of the "No Name Series" by Roberts Brothers of Boston. Under the editorship of Thomas Niles this well-known firm proposed to bring out a series of anonymous books, written, as the circular advertised, by American authors, "each a great unknown." The idea of making readers share in a guessing-game proved one of the most financially rewarding publishing schemes of the decade. *Mercy Philbrick's Choice* was widely reviewed as soon as it appeared, and some critics correctly guessed that Helen Hunt Jackson was the author. Neither she nor Niles the publisher confirmed the speculation or denied it.

Some biographers have seen in the incidents and plot of this latest novel by Mrs. Jackson further parallels with the career of Emily Dickinson. There are landmarks and names which identify Amherst as the setting. Mercy Philbrick is a soulful, gifted lady who becomes a distinguished poet. Her life is shaped by a devoted tutor and an older, retired clergyman to whom Mercy was more than a pupil — "she was also a warm and glowing personality, a young and beautiful woman." But the resemblances are generalized and vague, and one can with equal ease find semblances between Mercy and Helen Jackson herself. The book is a fictionalized projection of many composites from the author's imagination. Since Mrs. Jackson wrote it before she met Emily Dickinson, she would have felt no compunction in drawing upon hearsay to give events in Mercy's career some indeterminate resemblance to those hypothesized in Emily's.

Attributed to Lavinia, the story has spread that sometime during her widowhood Helen Hunt visited for two weeks in the Dickinson household and urged Emily to help write *Mercy Philbrick's Choice*, and that out of pique at Emily's refusal, worked her into the novel. The story is baseless. After Emily's death Vinnie labored with single-minded devotion to procure recognition of her sister's talents. Perhaps Vinnie really came to think the event occurred. More probably the story was imputed to her. Repeated assertion can give fabrication the status of actuality.

In all, some fourteen "No Names" were issued. Encouraged by Mrs. Jackson, Niles decided to bring out as a final volume an anthology of anonymous verse which would be contributed by American and English authors. The advertisements hinted that readers would encounter poems by Christina Rossetti, William Morris, Jean Ingelow, and "H.H." Such a collection would multiply the opportunity for speculation, and the volume, titled *A Masque of Poets*, appeared in 1878. It was one of the most profitable ventures Roberts Brothers ever undertook, and today, because it includes the first printing of one poem each by Thoreau, Lanier, and Dickinson, it is a collector's item. The meeting that took place in October 1876 came about because Helen Jackson was determined that Emily Dickinson should contribute to the proposed anthology.

The order of events touching upon the ultimate publication of the poem "Success" can be reconstructed from surviving letters. When in 1876 Emily Dickinson received Mrs. Jackson's letter of March twentieth, she answered it, complying with its request to

Rev. Charles Waasworth

Thomas Wentworth Higginson

Helen Hunt Jackson

The Holyoke Range seen from Amherst

send some poems. Receiving no acknowledgment from Mrs. Jackson, she wrote again during the summer to ask whether the silence meant that Mrs. Jackson was "offended." Over the many years of letter exchange with Colonel Higginson she had recurrently in brief notes asked such a question when she felt that his reply was overdue, always tempering her importunity by enclosing a poem. She wished to be an associate in the fellowship of busy authors like Colonel Higginson and Mrs. Jackson, but only as an inactive member. She had taken Mrs. Jackson's invitation to "write me now and then" with no more literalness than Mrs. Jackson had meant to give it, but with a different time sense.

On August twentieth Helen Jackson wrote from Princeton, Massachusetts, where she was again spending the summer. "My dear Miss Dickinson," she begins: "How could you possibly have offended me? I am sorry that such an idea should have suggested itself to you. I have often and often thought of sending you a line, but there are only sixty minutes to an hour. There are not half enough." She then gets to the point of her letter.

I enclose to you a circular which may interest you. When the volume of Verse is published in this series, I shall contribute to it: and I want to persuade you to. Surely, in the shelter of such *double* anonymousness as that will be, you need not shrink. I want to see some of your verses in print. Unless you forbid me, I will send some that I have. May I? — It will be some time before this volume appears. There ought to be three or four volumes of stories first, I suppose.

Pondering how to withhold consent without estranging this woman who kept making forthright requests, Emily Dickinson probably delayed a reply. Then on the tenth of October Mrs. Jackson arrived in Amherst and made a call to plead in person. Though Emily Dickinson recalled the interview with pleasure, at the time she must have been acutely uncomfortable, for she sat down immediately to ask help from the Colonel.

Dear friend — Are you willing to tell me what is right? Mrs Jackson — of Colorado — was with me a few moments this week, and wished me to write for this – I told her I was unwilling, and she asked me why? – I said I was incapable and she seemed not to believe me and asked me not to decide for a few Days – meantime, she would write me – She was so sweetly noble, I would regret to estrange her, and if you would be willing to give me a note saying you disapprove it, and thought me unfit, she would believe you – I am sorry to flee so often to my safest friend, but hope he permits me –

The circular must have been an early prospectus that said nothing about plans for a poetry anthology. Accepting with his habitual good grace the role of intercessor, her safest friend replied: "It is always hard to judge for another of the bent of inclination or range of talent; but I should not have thought of advising you to write stories, as it would not seem to me to be in your line. Perhaps Mrs. Jackson thought that the change & variety might be good for you: but if you really feel a strong unwillingness to attempt it, I don't think she would mean to urge you." It is expertly maneuvered between counsel and prescription, but unfortunately he was talking of stories only, and the reply therefore furnished no guidance on the question of how to deal with Mrs. Jackson.

Meanwhile Helen Jackson, who sensed that she had been carried away by her impetuousness, wrote from Ashfield, Massachusetts. She begins by apologizing for having remarked to Miss Dickinson that she lived away from sunlight:

. . . but truly you seemed so white and moth-like [and] your hand felt like such a wisp in mine that you frightened me — I felt like a great ox, talking to a white moth and begging it to come and eat grass with me to see if it could turn itself into beef! How stupid. —

This morning I have read over again the last verses you sent me: I find them more clear than I·thought they were. Part of the dimness must have been in me. Yet I have others which I like better . . . You say you find great pleasure in reading my verses. Let somebody somewhere whom you do not know have the same pleasure in reading yours.

The interview had given further substance to their friendship, but it had tended to strengthen rather than weaken Emily Dickinson's resolve not to consent to publication. Her letter to Colonel Higginson shortly thereafter confirms her decision: "Mrs Jackson has written. It was not stories she asked of me. But may I tell her just the same that you don't prefer it? Thank you, if I may, for it almost seems sordid to refuse from myself again."

Whether or not she mustered courage to invoke the sanction of the Colonel, the fact is that the subject of a contribution lapsed for eighteen months. Meanwhile during that fall or winter Emily Dickinson wrote a letter which again Mrs. Jackson did not answer. She waited for an interval, then wrote again to ask if Mrs. Jackson's face was "averted." This letter enclosed, in lieu of a poem one surmises, a photograph of two-year-old Gilbert. It was the act of an adoring aunt, but Mrs. Jackson must have wondered just what special emotion the enclosure was intended to elicit. The letter stung Mrs. Jackson into reply. From Colorado Springs on 29 April 1878 she wrote:

My face was not 'averted' in the least. It was only that I did not speak: and of my not speaking, I ought to be very much ashamed, and should be, if I had not got past being ashamed of my delinquencies in the matter of letter writing.

She chats amicably, then goes on:

Would it be of any use to ask you once more for one or two of your poems, to come out in the volume of "no name" poetry which is to be published before long by Roberts Bros.? If you will give me permission I will copy them — sending them in my own handwriting — and promise never to tell anyone, not even the publishers, whose the poems are. Could you not bear this much of publicity? Only you and I would recognize the poems. I wish very much you would do this — and I think you would have much amusement in seeing to whom the critics, those shrewd guessers, would ascribe your verses.

She expects to come East with her husband later in the year, she says, and asks to be remembered to a friend: "I was about to say 'When you see him,' but you never see anybody! Perhaps however you have improved. I send back the little baby face to tell you that I had not 'averted' my face — only the habit of speaking. It is an earnest and good little face: your brother's child I presume."

A Masque of Poets was scheduled for November publication, and copy should therefore be in the printer's hands immediately. As author Mrs. Jackson knew how to meet publishing deadlines, whatever her delinquencies as a letter writer. She had made up her mind that at least one Dickinson poem must be included. Emily was equally determined to withhold consent, and there the matter stood when the Jacksons came East in October. They arrived in Amherst during the week of the twenty-first, and Emily Dickinson received them for an hour one forenoon. Since *A Masque of Poets* was in fact on sale three weeks after this interview, one can only conclude that Mrs. Jackson had already supplied a copy of "Success," staking everything on this meeting and her persuasive arguments as the means of breaking down Emily Dickinson's determination not to publish. She failed.

The Jacksons left Amherst on Thursday the twenty-fourth, and on the following day Mrs. Jackson wrote a letter.

My dear friend — Here comes the line I promised to send . . . Now — will you send me the poem? No — will you let me send the "Success" — which I know by heart — to Roberts Bros for the Masque of Poets? If you will, it will give me great pleasure. I ask it as a personal favour to myself — Can you refuse the only thing I perhaps shall ever ask at your hands?

The plea is not a request; it is a cry for help which, of course, Emily Dickinson gave.

The call that the Jacksons had paid, Emily Dickinson pleasantly noted in a letter to Colonel Higginson and to Maria Whitney, a member of the modern language department at Smith College. She told Miss Whitney that the Jacksons had stopped in Springfield to see Mrs. Bowles, whose husband had died nine months before. "They found her, they said, a stricken woman, though not as ruthless as they feared." About this time she wrote an interesting quatrain.

How ruthless are the gentle
How cruel are the kind —
God broke his contract to his Lamb
To qualify the Wind —

It may have been suggested by the thought of Mary Bowles's condition. But the personal experience leading up to the publication
of "Success" tempts one to suspect a more intimate source of inspiration. With the best of intentions Mrs. Jackson had been very
importunate. On the other hand during the past two years Emily
Dickinson had been laying claims to Mrs. Jackson's attention that
were plainly self-indulgent. The sympathies of posterity will be
somewhat evenly divided.

In early December Mrs. Jackson wrote from Colorado Springs.

I suppose by this time you have seen the Masque of Poets. I hope
you have not regretted giving me that choice bit of verse for it. I was
pleased to see that it had in a manner, a special place, being chosen to
end the first part of the volume, — on the whole, the volume is a dis-
appointment to me. Still I think it has much interest for all literary
people. I confess myself quite unable to conjecture the authorship of
most of the poems.

She chats about the pleasant Colorado winter weather and concludes that she is glad they could meet again, "also that you saw
my husband and liked him, as I perceived that you did."

Helen Jackson had managed to include Emily Dickinson among
the contemporary poets, albeit with but one poem, and that one
anonymous. She had entered a wedge. Perhaps later she would
have less difficulty in persuading Emily Dickinson to issue a small
volume of poems. Six years later she tried again, but she died before
she had succeeded. And even had she lived, one can see that her
chances of success were visionary.

Helen Jackson was the intermediary through whom Thomas
Niles, the editor of Roberts Brothers, had been able to secure the
Dickinson poem. She thus was indirectly responsible for the spate
of correspondence that passed between Emily Dickinson and Niles

after the poem was published. Niles, who had started his career with the firm of Ticknor, had been with Roberts Brothers since 1862. Until his death in 1894 he served with distinction, and during his editorship the firm of Roberts Brothers, though not large, gained a reputation for the quality of its authors, both English and American.

Niles saw to it that a copy of *A Masque of Poets* was sent to Emily Dickinson, who wrote to thank him. He was aware of the many editorial changes in her poem, and used the opportunity of her reply to write a note to her in January 1879, assuming responsibility for the alterations. "You were entitled to a copy of 'A Masque of Poets,'" he said, "without thanks, for your valuable contribution which for want of a known sponsor Mr Emerson has generally had to father. I wanted to send you a proof of your poem, wh. as you have doubtless perceived was slightly changed in phraseology." The attribution was very high praise indeed. She had been compelled to bypass the chance to edit her poem in all probability because Niles may never have been sure until after publication that Mrs. Jackson's stratagem had worked. Yet from her point of view changes had been made, and without her permission. This latest evidence of editorial highhandedness was in line with her past experience, but this time the changes must have been exasperating.

Written in 1859, the poem "Success" was one that she had sent to Colonel Higginson in 1862. Mrs. Jackson's letters imply that the transcript she used she had had for some time, and one infers that she made it from the copy that Higginson possessed. There are three surviving fair copies of the poem, all identical in text. One presumes therefore that the transcript given to Niles read thus:

> Success is counted sweetest
> By those who ne'er succeed.
> To comprehend a nectar
> Requires sorest need.
>
> Not one of all the purple host
> Who took the flag today

Can tell the definition
So clear of Victory

As he defeated — dying —
On whose forbidden ear
The distant strains of triumph
Burst agonized and clear!

Niles introduced five alterations: 2. who] that; 3. a nectar] the
nectar; 4. sorest] the sorest; 8. clear] plain; 12] Break, agonizing
clear.

Since protest was now useless, an irritated riposte would be un-
mannerly, whether written to Niles or Mrs. Jackson. Friendships
were important. By the end of the year 1878 the letter exchange
between the two women enters a new phase of untroubled cordiality. Typical of the spirit is the poem written late that year or early
in the next, seemingly a note asking news of Mrs. Jackson.

Spurn the temerity —
Rashness of Calvary —
Gay were Gethsemane
Knew we of Thee —

Helen Jackson sent it to Colonel Higginson (who kept it) with the
notation beneath: "Wonderful twelve words!" Her insight was better than her word count.

Also about this time Emily Dickinson wrote a poem on the bluebird, the one beginning "Before you thought of spring." It is one of
the charming portraits of aspects of nature which in these years she
enjoyed writing because she had mastered a new genre. Sometime
in the spring of 1879 she sent a copy of it to Mrs. Jackson, who on
May twelfth engagingly acknowledged it:

I know your "Blue bird" by heart — and that is more than I do of any
of my own verses. I also want your permission to send it to Col. Higginson to read. These two things are my testimonial to its merit. We have
blue birds here — I might have had the sense to write something about
one myself, but I never did: and now I never can. For which I am in-

clined to envy, and perhaps hate you . . . What should you think of trying your hand on the oriole? He will be along presently.

She adds a postscript: "Write & tell me if I may pass the Blue Bird along to the Col?"

The idea of trying her hand on the oriole struck her fancy and she wrote "One of the ones that Midas touched," the seven-stanza poem that transmutes the bird's dazzling, reeling splendor into poetry. This she sent to Mrs. Jackson, adding "A Route of Evanescence": "To the Oriole you suggested I add a Humming Bird and hope they are not untrue."

During the summer of 1879 Higginson got together a series of brief essays which he titled *Short Studies of American Authors*. The book devotes about ten pages each to Hawthorne, Poe, Thoreau, Howells, Henry James, and Helen Jackson. Advertised as a "holiday book," it sold for fifty cents and was intended to catch the Christmas trade. Higginson sent a copy of it to Emily Dickinson as a seasonal greeting. Her letter of acknowledgment comments on some of the authors. "Of Poe, I know too little to think," she says, meaning evidently that she did not care for him. "Hawthorne appalls, entices" seems to say that she found Hawthorne's somber themes dismaying, but was attracted to them by his artistry. She comments that "of Howells and James, one hesitates." She probably did not care for the realism of Howells or the prolixity of James. She has nothing to say about Thoreau, although Higginson's criticism is sound and warmly sympathetic.

It is worth notice that all her literary judgments, expressed in that letter and in others, strikingly parallel opinions held by Dr. Holland. As a friend of the Doctor, and as a close reader of his *Scribner's Monthly*, she may well have allowed her taste to be guided by his, especially in judgments about current writers. He approved of Hawthorne, had no patience with Poe and Thoreau, and felt uneasy with Howells and James. Only once did Emily Dickinson ever mention Thoreau, and then in a letter written to Sue back in 1866, after Sue had been at the seashore: "Was the

Sea cordial? Kiss him for Thoreau." Just what critical estimate is implied would be hard to say.

Only in her comment on Higginson's appreciation of Helen Jackson does she speak without a reservation: "Mrs Jackson soars to your estimation lawfully as a Bird." Higginson finds analogies for Mrs. Jackson's poetry with that of Andrew Marvell and Henry Vaughan, and calls her "the woman who has come nearest in our day and tongue to the genius of Elizabeth Barrett Browning." He goes on to tell the story of how Emerson, when asked whether he did not think "H.H." the best woman-poet on the continent, replied: "Perhaps we might as well omit the *woman*." Emerson, he says, "used to cut her poems from the newspapers as they appeared, to carry them about with him, and to read them aloud." If Higginson's estimate seems inflated, what are we to think of Emerson's? Emerson increasingly seems to have had truer sensibilities than most critics of his day, yet one finds difficulty in reconciling his reported judgment with the essential mediocrity of Mrs. Jackson's verses. Emily Dickinson's appraisal certainly was intended seriously, and was sustained by the critics and the public alike. Eight years earlier she had given Higginson her opinion, likewise singling out Mrs. Browning for comparison: "Mrs Hunt's Poems are stronger than any written by Women since Mrs. Browning, with the exception of Mrs Lewes [George Eliot]." The fact is that Emily Dickinson had little interest in the art of criticism, and her judgment of others' talents, especially among her contemporaries, does not strike one today as being either original or deeply perceptive. She was a poet, not a critic.

From 1879 until the year of her death Helen Jackson was a bird of passage, restlessly alighting now in Maine and Boston, Europe and New York, Oregon and Mexico, California and Colorado Springs, though she never stopped again in Amherst. She was writing with such prolific energy that four of her books — stories, essays, and poems — were posthumously issued. Her life in the West had given focus to new interests. She undertook a study of the govern-

ment's dealings with Indian tribes, and after several months of re-
search at the Astor Library in New York City, using the great resources of the John Jacob Astor collection of western Americana,
she published in 1881 an important 457-page tract entitled *A Century of Dishonor*, a documented indictment of jurisdictional treachery. Not satisfied with the effect of her report, which won her a
special government commission, she decided to point up her story
by telling it as a novel. She did so in *Ramona* (1884), her finest
work as a writer, and the one by which she is still remembered.
Engrossed in these concerns, she had little time to spare for casual
letter writing, and the Jackson-Dickinson correspondence, brief as
it had been, came virtually to an end. It flared vividly for a moment
shortly before her death, but ties of any personal sort, which never
had been close, were broken. Emily sent her a note in April 1883,
enclosing pressed flowers, said to be bluebells, with two brief lines
of verse saying that Mrs. Jackson was not forgotten, but any reply
at this time is unlikely.

In the meantime pressure on Emily Dickinson to publish came
from a new source. In April 1882 she wrote Thomas Niles to inquire when Cross's *Life of George Eliot*, announced for publication,
could be expected. He answered her question, and then took the
opportunity to add as a final paragraph: "'H.H.' once told me that
she wished you could be induced to publish a volume of poems. I
should not want to say how highly she praised them, but to such
an extent that I wish also that you could." She acknowledged his
letter, concluding: "The kind but incredible opinion of 'H.H.' and
yourself I would like to deserve. Would you accept a Pebble I think
I gave to her, though I am not sure." The enclosure was this poem.

> How happy is the little Stone
> That rambles in the Road alone,
> And does'nt care about Careers
> And Exigencies never fears –
> Whose Coat of elemental Brown
> A passing Universe put on,
> And independent as the Sun

Associates or glows alone,
Fulfilling absolute Decree
In casual simplicity –

Perhaps she thought that he would take the poem as a reply to his final paragraph.

A year later she renewed her inquiry about Cross's *Life*. Niles replied that he had heard no more about it, but that Roberts Brothers was about to publish a biography of George Eliot by Mathilde Blind. He arranged to have her sent a copy which she acknowledged with a note enclosing "Further in Summer than the Birds" and "It sifts from Leaden Sieves" – poems that she designated by title as "My Cricket" and "The Snow." Like all selections of poems that she sent to friends in the later years, both deal with aspects of nature. These particular ones had been composed many years before, during the sixties. She took a further step to match his kindness, and sent him her own 1848 copy of the Brontë sisters' poems. Her impulsive act gave Niles the opportunity for which he had apparently been waiting. On 31 March 1883, he replied:

I received the copy of "Currer, Ellis & Acton Bells Poems." I already have a copy of a later Ed. which contains all of these and additional poems by Ellis & Acton.

Surely you did not mean to present me with your copy – if you did, I thank you heartily, but in doing so I must add that I would not for the world rob you of this very rare book, of which this is such a nice copy.

If I may presume to say so, I will take instead a M.S. collection of your poems, that is, if you want to give them to the world through the medium of a publisher.

And he added in postscript: "I return the precious little volume by mail." Her reply to his offer merely thanks him "for the kindness," but it included three more poems, which Niles immediately acknowledged: "I am very much obliged to you for the three poems which I have read & reread with great pleasure, but which I have not consumed. I shall keep them unless you order me to do otherwise – in that case I shall as in duty bound obey." The three, as she knew, were among her finest: "A Route of Evanescence," "Ample make this Bed," and "The Wind begun to rock the Grass."

The interlude of the Niles-Dickinson correspondence had been brought about by Helen Jackson, and it had been continued by virtue of Mrs. Jackson's oft-repeated conviction that Emily Dickinson was a great poet. It now came to an end because Niles had found out, as Mrs. Jackson was shortly to do, that a renewal of his offer to publish was useless, since Emily Dickinson could not be induced to give her poetry to the world.

Seven years later, after Emily Dickinson's death, and at the time Mrs. Todd and Colonel Higginson were editing for Roberts Brothers the first volume of Dickinson *Poems*, Niles expressed an opinion to Higginson which makes curious reading in the light of his earlier firm offer to Emily Dickinson to publish a volume of her poetry. His literary advisor in 1890 was the editor and novelist Arlo Bates, who told Niles that in his opinion Emily Dickinson had no technique, and that if Niles intended to publish any of her verse he should exercise careful selection. Niles amplified Bates's dispraise thus in a letter to Higginson in June 1890: "It has always seemed to me that it would be unwise to perpetuate Miss Dickinson's poems. They are quite as remarkable for defects as for beauties & are generally devoid of true poetical qualities." Such an about-face is in part a measure of Niles's singular critical limitations, but the statement should probably be read as a shrewd bargaining proposal rather than a literary opinion. If the firm contracted to publish the poems, it intended to compel Lavinia Dickinson to pay for the plates, and such indeed was the arrangement by which the poems were issued.

Helen Jackson, who was in New York late in 1883, commenced *Ramona* in December and concluded it during the spring of 1884. The concentrated effort left her nervously exhausted, and as soon as she could do so she left for Colorado Springs. In consequence of a fall down a flight of stairs, resulting in a broken leg, she was on crutches for many months. Upon learning of the injury, Emily

Dickinson wrote a note of sympathy. Mrs. Jackson's reply is dated September fifth. Chatty and gay in spite of her restrictions, she gives details of the injury and of her life in a wheelchair. Then she adds:

What portfolios of verses you must have. — It is a cruel wrong to your "day & generation" that you will not give them light. — If such a thing should happen as that I should outlive you, I wish you would make me your literary legatee & executor. Surely, after you are what is called "dead," you will be willing that the poor ghosts you have left behind, should be cheered and pleased by your verses, will you not? — You ought to be. — I do not think we have a right to with hold from the world a word or a thought any more than a *deed*, which might help a single soul.

The sententiousness of the letter Emily Dickinson could forgive because the opinion expressed was so translucently honest. The mood of her reply reflects the stimulus that such a letter supplied.

Dear friend — I infer from your Note you have "taken Captivity Captive," and rejoice that that martial Verse has been verified. He who is "slain and smiles, steals something from the" Sword, but you have stolen the Sword itself, which is far better — I hope you may be harmed no more — I shall watch your passage from Crutch to Cane with jealous affection. From there to your Wings is but a stride — as was said of the convalescing Bird,

> And then he lifted up his Throat
> And squandered such a Note —
> A Universe that overheard
> Is stricken by it yet —

I, too, took my summer in a Chair, though from "Nervous prostration," not fracture, but take my Nerve by the Bridle now, and am again abroad — Thank you for the wish —

The summer has been wide and deep, and a deeper Autumn is but the Gleam concomitant of that waylaying Light —

> Pursuing you in your transitions,
> In other Motes —
> Of other Myths

Your requisition be.
The Prism never held the Hues,
It only heard them play –

And she signs herself, "Loyally, E. Dickinson."

There are two interesting features about the letter. The issue of publication and executorship is pointedly ignored; and Mrs. Jackson forwarded the letter to Colonel Higginson, for it now rests among his papers. Her intent in so doing must have been merely to bring the poems to his attention, for he did not learn of Mrs. Jackson's request to act as literary legatee until Lavinia discovered Mrs. Jackson's letter in 1891.

Helen Jackson recovered more slowly than she expected. Writing Emily Dickinson in February 1885, she chats at length about her domestic routine: ". . . but [I] dare not grumble, lest a worse thing befall me: & if I did grumble, I should deserve it, – for I am absolutely well – drive the whole of every afternoon in an open carriage on roads where larks sing & flowers are in bloom: I can do everything I ever could – except walk!" She cannot resist one concluding remark about the poetry: "I hope you are well – and at work – I wish I knew what your portfolios, by this time, hold." Emily Dickinson's reply in March, incorporating two poems, loyally comments: "Pity me, however, I have just finished *Ramona*. Would that like Shakespeare it were just published!"

Not her injury, but cancer, was the cause of Mrs. Jackson's steady decline. As a last resort she was removed to San Francisco where she lingered on until August twelfth. Emily Dickinson learned about the impending death from a newspaper account. This she clipped and enclosed in a letter to Colonel Higginson. "I was unspeakably shocked to see this in the Morning Paper – She wrote me in Spring that she could not walk, but not that she would die. . . What a Hazard a Letter is! When I think of the Hearts it has scuttled and sunk – I almost fear to lift my Hand to so much as a Superscription." Later in the month she sent a letter of condolence to Mr. Jackson, and at the same time she wrote Thomas Niles to inquire what details he knew, and to secure a photograph if possible. Niles replied shortly, adding: "In her last letter to me, recd. since the news of her death, she says she 'has but a few days to live and shall be thankful to be released' and she closes thus: 'I shall look in on your new rooms some day, be sure — but you won't see me — Good bye — Affy. forever. H. J.' "

The last two letters that Emily Dickinson wrote to Colonel Higginson shortly before her own death, when she herself must have had some premonition, deal solely with her great admiration for Helen Jackson.

When she came the last time she had in her Hand as I entered, [George Eliot's] the "Choir invisible." "Superb," she said as she shut the Book, stooping to receive me, but fervor suffocates me – Thank you for "the Sonnet" — I have lain it at her loved feet —

> Not knowing when Herself may come
> I open every Door,
> Or has she Feathers, like a Bird,
> Or Billows, like a Shore —

The sonnet to which she refers Higginson had written in memory of Mrs. Jackson, and it was published in the *Century Magazine* for May. In all probability he sent Emily Dickinson a copy in advance of publication. Two other brief elegies she incorporated in a later letter.

The reasons for her emotion, almost an adoration of Helen Jackson, Higginson could not fully know. But Helen Jackson had given Emily Dickinson, as no other person ever did, a conviction that her poems were of first importance. Nothing ever touched her more deeply than the recognition thus bestowed upon her art — and by another poet, one whom the best critics of the day acclaimed as a leading, if not the leading, writer of verse in America.

Sometime about 1881 Emily set down in worksheet draft a poem which is finished only in its first stanza.

Above Oblivion's Tide there is a Pier
And an effaceless "Few" are lifted there –
Nay – lift themselves – Fame has no Arms –
And but one smile – that meagres Balms –

One easily understands why she was dissatisfied with the result as poetry, but the lines show the degree to which she came to perceive that the "Few" lift themselves. Though Helen Jackson never understood why her offices were declined, she had assisted in nameless ways. Among them she had given Emily Dickinson a conviction that she did not need the arms of Fame to lift her.

Part Three

FLOOD SUBJECTS

VIII

NATURE: The Haunted House

WHEN EMILY DICKINSON told Colonel Higginson that "Nature is a Haunted House – but Art a House that tries to be haunted," she was ostensibly saying that art imitates nature. But the implication of the remark goes further, because it gives a clue to her concept of nature itself. For her, the world of nature is a dwelling place, hauntingly mysterious, peopled with God's creatures who live amid the phenomena God ordains and regulates. In 1863 she explicitly defined nature in terms of sensation.

> "Nature" is what we see –
> The Hill – the Afternoon –
> Squirrel – Eclipse – the Bumble bee –
> Nay – Nature is Heaven –
> Nature is what we hear –
> The Bobolink – the Sea –
> Thunder – the Cricket –
> Nay – Nature is Harmony –
> Nature is what we know –
> Yet have no art to say –
> So impotent Our Wisdom is
> To her Simplicity

It is the things we see, hear, and feel. It is the harmonious coexistence of all things as we observe them by our senses and our intuition. She feels that it is "Heaven" to be alive and dwell in a house near so many fascinating creatures, moods, and vistas.

Most of the nature poems evoke moods or describe scenes wherein the creatures or the phenomena of the world about us are central to her thought. Nature as a symbol of the processes by which death gives us immortality is the subject of a great body of her poetry, but she does not have that process in mind as she defines the word. Nor does she mean by it a correspondence between man and the cosmos, or between the Creator and the creature. God, man, and nature she sharply differentiates. Nature cannot be explained any more easily than God can be explained, but both can be personified.

> Nature and God – I neither knew
> Yet Both so well knew me
> They startled, like Executors
> Of My identity
>
> Yet Neither told – that I could learn –
> My Secret as secure
> As Herschel's private interest
> Or Mercury's affair –

Nature is a separate entity, made privy to the Creator's secrets which are not revealed to any man.

As Creator, God ordains, and man is directly under his governance. But God has deputized his authority in dealing with all his other creatures. Their welfare is made the sole concern of Nature, a spirit which is personified as the gentlest of mothers. Emily Dickinson pictured her thus in 1863, in a six-stanza poem:

> Nature – the Gentlest Mother is,
> Impatient of no Child –
> The feeblest – or the waywardest –
> Her Admonition mild –
>
> In Forest – and the Hill –
> By Traveller – be heard –
> Restraining Rampant Squirrel –
> Or too impetuous Bird –

Her vigilance never relaxes, and the least in her family is moved to adoration by the love which her voice incites.

NATURE

How fair Her Conversation –
A Summer Afternoon –
Her Household – Her Assembly –
And when the Sun go down –

Her Voice among the Aisles
Incite the timid prayer
Of the minutest Cricket –
The most unworthy Flower –

When at night her children sleep, she lights her lamps and bends
from the sky to whisper a benediction.

When all the Children sleep –
She turns as long away
As will suffice to light Her lamps –
Then bending from the Sky –

With infinite Affection –
And infiniter Care –
Her Golden finger on Her lip –
Wills Silence – Everywhere –

This is one of the very few poems in which personified Nature
is as central in the picture as the brood which she tends. Usually
Emily Dickinson focuses attention upon the creatures in Nature's
charge or the moods created by Nature. Thus Nature generally remains a benign but unapproachable spirit, inspiring awe in man
and receiving the adoration of those in her care. As creatures in
nature, the crickets quite properly should offer a prayer to their
mother.

Most of the nature poems sketch the creatures she knew or the
moods of the days or the seasons. She was especially moved by contemplation of spring or summer, for they are the months of expectation and of nature's fulfillment. One of the finest of the nature
lyrics was written about 1866. It is not a meditation on death, as
it sometimes has been thought to be. It attempts to conjure up
that moment in late summer when the beholder is given a premoni-
tory warning that summer is slipping away. The sudden realization

of the fact — the first indeed that the beholder has had — comes as a dispiriting surprise. Nothing in nature yet is visibly altered, but the poet, because she now apprehends the truth, is changed. As in the earlier poem, crickets worship Mother Nature, but are made more central to the theme. She titled the poem "My Cricket."

> Further in Summer than the Birds
> Pathetic from the Grass
> A minor Nation celebrates
> It's unobtrusive Mass.
>
> No Ordinance be seen
> So gradual the Grace
> A pensive Custom it becomes
> Enlarging Loneliness.
>
> Antiquest felt at Noon
> When August burning low
> Arise this spectral Canticle
> Repose to typify
>
> Remit as yet no Grace
> No Furrow on the Glow
> Yet a Druidic Difference
> Enhances Nature now

Crickets arrive later in the summer than the birds do, and their song, warning us of summer's departure, is afflictive. Together and as a group they offer a High Mass to their Mother. We hear but cannot see them at their communion. The change of season (Grace) from summer to autumn is so gradual that only such a sign as the chirping of crickets brings the change to our notice. We muse upon the fact sadly, for each year that passes increases the loneliness that we feel for things irrevocably gone. These long, long thoughts (Antiquest) seem to tie the present to all pasts at the very moment (Noon) when the day seems most golden. The cricket songs remind us of, indeed they typify, the repose that Nature will take in her long winter sleep. Yet August is still at full, and glancing about we see no sign that the season is changing (Remit as yet no Grace). No furrow yet crosses the glow of summer. Yet by an occult signal (for how do crickets know when their predestined moment to chirp has arrived?) we are warned that summer is passing. Thus our enjoyment of nature at the full is enlarged.

The idea, in all its complex subtlety, is encompassed in fewer than seventy words. The rhyme is exact in the beginning, becomes irregular in the second stanza, where the loneliness is emphasized, disappears in the third, where the thought is projected into both past and future, and reappears at the end, linking the two final stanzas, the fourth contrasting with the third by dealing solely with the present. The Common Meter of the first stanza is thereafter abandoned for the more spare Short Meter. One word in each stanza ties all stanzas together in a mood of anxiety: *pathetic, pensive, spectral, enhances.* The long, long thoughts are borne by *antiquest* and *Druidic,* words suggesting things in a dim past. The awe is made solemn by the act of communion, the word *canticle,* and the phrase "Druidic Difference." In such poems as this Emily Dickinson shows mastery not only in form but in the utterance itself. She does not make her emotional experience the end in view. Her intuition takes her below the surface of the experience into the heart of all such moments of sensation.

The poet's growth as an artist is strikingly apparent when the poem above is examined beside one written about 1859 on the theme of Indian summer.

> These are the days when Birds come back –
> A very few – a Bird or two –
> To take a backward look.
>
> These are the days when skies resume
> The old – old sophistries of June –
> A blue and gold mistake.
>
> Oh fraud that cannot cheat the Bee –
> Almost thy plausibility
> Induces my belief.

Till ranks of seeds their witness bear –
And softly thro' the altered air
Hurries a timid leaf.

Oh Sacrament of summer days,
Oh Last Communion in the Haze –
Permit a child to join.

Thy sacred emblems to partake –
Thy consecrated bread to take
And thine immortal wine!

The poem has charm because the poet communicates the fervor of her enthusiasm. She bids summer farewell by participating in the rites which here also are a communion. She uses the Common Particular meter and her rhymes are exact. She follows the eighteenth-century tradition, common in hymnals today, that gives *join* and *wine* the same vowel sound. But here her own emotional experience is the sole end in view. The fact that her knowledge of entomology happens to be inexact is beside the point: bees will gather honey whenever they find it. But the images are vague and generalized. She wishes to join in the rite as "Emilie," a child, and the stress of her emotion leads her to transfer her own timidity to the falling leaf.

She essayed the same theme many years later, about 1877, and the picture is sharply in focus.

A field of Stubble, lying sere
Beneath the second Sun –
It's Toils to Brindled People thrust –
It's Triumphs – to the Bin –
Accosted by a timid Bird
Irresolute of Alms –
Is often seen – but seldom felt,
On our New England Farms –

She is not looking up into the hazy distance, but down at the good earth. Here is the realism of stubble and a dried-out field. Corn is thrust to cattle, and pumpkins are put in bins. The emotion is not a swoon but a lively identification of herself with the soil, with labor performed and food and fodder laid up for the winter.

Each season of the year gave her occasion for extracting the essence of a mood. She devoted the fewest poems to winter.

> Like Brooms of Steel
> The Snow and Wind
> Had swept the Winter Street —
> The House was hooked
> The Sun sent out
> Faint Deputies of Heat —
> Where rode the Bird
> The Silence tied
> His ample — plodding Steed
> The Apple in the Cellar snug
> Was all the one that played.

The picture is in the genre tradition. Bare streets, houses closed against the cold, a faint sun, a lone bird, and silence constitute the vista and mood outside, a mood reflected within as well, for we see only the storage bin in the winter cellar. But the objects are solid and the place is Amherst.

Her dread of winter she expressed in one of her remarkable verses, written about 1861. It is, like the somewhat later "Further in Summer than the Birds," an attempt to give permanence through her art to the impermanent; to catch that fleeting moment of anxiety which, having passed, leaves the beholder changed. Such moods she could catch most readily in the changing seasons themselves.

> There's a certain Slant of light,
> Winter Afternoons —
> That oppresses, like the Heft
> Of Cathedral Tunes —
>
> Heavenly Hurt, it gives us —
> We can find no scar,
> But internal difference,
> Where the Meanings, are —

None may teach it – Any –
'Tis the Seal Despair –
An imperial affliction
Sent us of the Air –

When it comes, the Landscape listens –
Shadows – hold their breath –
When it goes, 'tis like the Distance
On the look of Death –

Winter to her is at moments intolerably dreary, and she here re-
creates the actual emotion implicit in the Persephone-Pluto myth.
Will spring never come? Sometimes, winter afternoons, she perceives an atmospheric quality of light that is intensely oppressive.
The colloquial expression "heft" is especially appropriate in suggesting a heavy weight, which she associates with the weight of
great bells or the heavy sound that great bells create. This might
be the depressing chill and quiet preceding a snowfall. Whatever
it is, it puts the seal on wintriness. Coming as it does from heavens,
it is an imperial affliction to be endured ("None may teach it –
Any"). Even the landscape itself is depressed. When it leaves, she
feels that something has been withdrawn that had the imperturba-
ble, impersonal, unfeeling, unseeing "look" on the face of the dead
– or on the face of the king of the underworld whence she cannot
be rescued until spring.

Her own uncertainty when that moment can be expected is
reflected in the metric fluctuation. The stanzas are trochaic, and no
two have the same number of feet: Sevens and Fives, Sixes and
Fives, Eights and Fives, and, in the third stanza combination of the
second and third group. The rhymes, after the first, are coldly exact;
and throughout we are made to feel the weight of the gloom through
the language itself: *oppresses, heft, hurt, scar, despair, affliction,*
and "the look of Death."

With the coming of spring Emily Dickinson's spirit burgeoned
even as the world of nature about her.

The Notice that is called the Spring
Is but a month from here –

NATURE

> Put up my Heart thy Hoary work
> And take a Rosy Chair.

Or again:

> I cannot meet the Spring unmoved –
> I feel the old desire –
> A Hurry with a lingering, mixed,
> A Warrant to be fair –

It is, as she called it, a period express from God, a magical frontier.

> A Light exists in Spring
> Not present on the Year
> At any other period –

It cannot be described.

> It passes and we stay –
> A quality of loss
> Affecting our Content
> As Trade had suddenly encroached
> Upon a Sacrament.

March — "the Month of Expectation" — she made the subject of five poems; this is typical:

> We like March – his shoes are Purple.
> He is new and high –
> Makes he Mud for Dog and Peddler –
> Makes he Forests Dry –
> Knows the Adders Tongue his coming
> And begets her spot –
> Stands the Sun so close and mighty –
> That our Minds are hot.
> News is he of all the others –
> Bold it were to die
> With the Blue Birds buccaneering
> On his British sky –

Perhaps she captured the feeling of exuberant well-being best in these haunting lines.

FLOOD SUBJECTS

A little Madness in the Spring
Is wholesome even for the King.
But God be with the Clown –
Who ponders this tremendous scene –
This whole Experiment of Green –
As if it were his own!

Emily Dickinson's observation of creatures and the phenomena of the seasons is most lively when she sees them out-of-doors and in motion. Her association with the world of nature was an unalloyed happiness. The anxiety in her communion with friends is always very evident. "Are friends delight or pain?" is a question she never thought of asking about the inheritors of garden, tree, and stream. The creatures she depicts are either at play or occupied with the business of living, which in itself for them is pleasure. Even when a gale or a thunderstorm lashes with fury, it does so with no fell intent to make life difficult for mortals, but only because the nature of a gale is to blow fiercely, or of lightning to connect with something. An exception is apparent in her poem on the frost, because frost destroys and is associated with winter. Frost is intentionally cruel. He moves like a ghost and gives the kiss of death. He corresponds in the world of nature to the character of Death that she created and made the suitor of mortals.

A Visitor in Marl –
Who influences Flowers –
Till they are orderly as Busts –
And Elegant – as Glass –

Who visits in the Night –
And just before the Sun –
Concludes his glistening interview –
Caresses – and is gone –

But whom his fingers touched –
And where his feet have run –
And whatsoever Mouth he kissed –
Is as it had not been –

Though she disliked winter, she accepted it as fact, and could create an animated scene of falling snow. But, like frost, snow is predatory.

It sifts from Leaden Sieves –
It powders all the Wood.
It fills with Alabaster Wool
The Wrinkles of the Road –

It makes an Even Face
Of Mountain, and of Plain –
Unbroken Forehead from the East
Unto the East again –

It reaches to the Fence –
It wraps it Rail by Rail
Till it is lost in Fleeces –
It deals Celestial Vail

To Stump, and Stack – and Stem –
A Summer's empty Room –
Acres of Joints, where Harvests were,
Recordless, but for them –

It Ruffles Wrists of Posts
As Ankles of a Queen –
Then stills it's Artisans – like Ghosts –
Denying they have been –

The mood here, especially in the final stanza, is very much akin to that created in the poem on the frost. Snow is not here associated with gay sledding parties or snowball fights. The poem is a still-life picture. The eye is made to sweep the full circumference of the horizon, starting in the east. Trees, roads, hills, and meadows are in the background; in the middle distance a fence, stump, hay-stack, and sere stem. Nowhere are people to be seen.

Since thunderstorms are phenomena of summer, they are associated with the loved season, and her best description of one such storm is lively and unterrified.

The Wind begun to knead the Grass –
As Women do a Dough –
He flung a Hand full at the Plain –
A Hand full at the Sky –
The Leaves unhooked themselves from Trees –
And started all abroad –
The Dust did scoop itself like Hands –
And throw away the Road –
The Wagons quickened on the Street –
The Thunders gossiped low –
The Lightning showed a Yellow Head –
And then a livid Toe –
The Birds put up the Bars to Nests –
The Cattle flung to Barns –
Then came one drop of Giant Rain –
And then, as if the Hands
That held the Dams – had parted hold –
The Waters Wrecked the Sky –
But overlooked my Father's House –
Just Quartering a Tree –

Here is activity aplenty. One associates the poem, not with Lear's heath, but with a Breughel painting. People as well as all the creatures of the country are in the picture. One cannot take too seriously thunder that gossips or lightning that seems to be doing a polka. To be sure, a tree was quartered, but "my Father's House" was spared. While it lasted the storm was exciting, and no one really was harmed.

She was alert each day to the varying moods of nature. Two of her best realized nature poems, one on the sunrise and one on the wind, she sent to Colonel Higginson: "I'll tell you how the Sun rose" and "Of all the Sounds despatched abroad." One need not multiply examples, for she found occasion for such poems in all the incidents she experienced: the day's appearance and departure, falling leaves, cloud effects, a rising moon, mountain shadows, or the sound of rain dripping from the eaves. One phenomenon observed by all nature lovers, but rarely a subject of verse, is that period of time in May and June when birds announce the dawn, breaking into a great chorus of song, then falling silent at sunrise. Emily Dickinson twice made it the subject of a poem. The first, in six stanzas, she wrote about 1862, but left in a semifinal state with suggested changes for many words and phrases. Evidently she felt she had not transmuted the elusive quality of sound, the crescendo and diminuendo of the chorus, into poetry. Four years later she returned to the theme, encompassing it this time in three stanzas.

> At Half past.Three, a single Bird
> Unto a silent Sky
> Propounded but a single term
> Of cautious melody.
>
> At Half past Four, Experiment
> Had subjugated test
> And lo, Her silver Principle
> Supplanted all the rest.
>
> At Half past Seven, Element
> Nor Implement, be seen –
> And Place was where the Presence was
> Circumference between.

She must have felt assurance that she had realized her intent, for the poem survives in four fair copies, identical in text, sent to friends.

Emily Dickinson once specified August as the month that had given her the most. Among other reasons was the fact that August is the month when summer is at full. During August 1880 she took occasion to write Colonel Higginson, simply to express her delight in the landscape that lay about her. The Higginsons had lost an infant daughter that spring, and she ties his memory of the child into the event she narrates.

> I was touchingly reminded of your little Louisa this Morning by an Indian Woman with gay Baskets and a dazzling Baby, at the Kitchen Door. Her little Boy "once died," she said, Death to her dispelling him.

I asked her what the Baby liked, and she said "to step." The Prairie before the Door was gay with Flowers of Hay, and I led her in. She argued with the Birds – she leaned on Clover Walls and they fell, and dropped her. With jargon sweeter than a Bell, she grappled Buttercups, and they sank together, the Buttercups the heaviest. What sweetest use of Days!

The tranquil restoration which such moments brought to William Wordsworth they brought to Emily Dickinson. It is significant that the circumstances reminded her not of Wordsworth, whose poetry she knew something about, but of Henry Vaughan, whom at this point in her letter she quotes: " 'Twas noting some such Scene made Vaughn humbly say 'My Days that are at best but dim and hoary – ' I think it was Vaughn." (The fact that Vaughan's name is misspelled and the line misquoted is something of a hint that Vaughan was a poet she greatly admired. She memorized passages from the writing of those poets who pleased her most: Shakespeare, for instance, and, among her contemporaries, Browning. But she never bothered to verify her quotations, and they are inexact.) It is unlikely that she knew Vaughan's poetry inspired Wordsworth's great "Ode on the Intimations of Immortality." The fact is that this letter testifies to her admiration for that seventeenth-century mystic, whose imagination stirred her own, and whose feeling for nature and the homely terms of everyday usage in which he dared to express it, she shared.

The seasons and the days play around us and force their attention on us because we must take account of their moods: wear boots in mud time, cover crops against an unseasonable chill, or close our ears to the chorus of birds on summer mornings when we wish to sleep. But Emily Dickinson did not choose to close her ears or eyes. In fact, she felt awe in looking at so commonplace an object as a well. "What mystery pervades a well!" she exclaims. Its waters live so far that they seem awesome, like neighbors from another world. Yet the grass beside the well shows no fear. Pondering the relation of things, she concludes:

But nature is a stranger yet;
The ones that cite her most
Have never passed the haunted house,
Nor simplified her ghost.

To pity those that know her not
Is helped by the regret
That those who know her, know her less
The nearer her they get.

On occasion her poems are in the tradition that records a mystical or philosophical sense of nature. The following she felt to be successful, for she sent copies of it to friends.

A Dew sufficed itself
And satisfied a Leaf –
And thought "How vast a destiny" –
"How trivial is Life!"

The Sun went out to work –
The Day went out to play –
But not again that Dew be seen
By Physiognomy.

Whether by Day abducted
Or emptied by the Sun
Into the Sea in passing –
Eternally unknown.

Attested to this Day
That awful Tragedy
By Transport's instability
And Doom's celerity.

But generally she approached her subjects like a genre painter, sketching realistically the scenes from everyday experience. Her deservedly well-known "Snake" is a "narrow fellow" whose notice is sudden. He divides the grass "as with a comb," and appears as a "spotted shaft."

He likes a Boggy Acre –
A Floor too cool for Corn –

The link with soil in which corn will not thrive is deft. She concludes that she knows and likes several of nature's people, but she
never meets this fellow

> Attended, or alone
> Without a tighter breathing
> And Zero at the Bone.

Some of her lyrics are written as studies, as études, built upon a
simple descriptive theme.

> The Robin is a Gabriel
> In humble circumstances –
> His Dress denotes him socially,
> Of Transport's Working Classes –
> He has the punctuality
> Of the New England Farmer –
> The same oblique integrity,
> A Vista vastly warmer –
>
> A small but sturdy Residence,
> A self denying Household,
> The Guests of Perspicacity
> Are all that cross his Threshold –
> As covert as a Fugitive,
> Cajoling Consternation
> By Ditties to the Enemy
> And Sylvan Punctuation –

Gabriel, the harbinger, has arrived punctually in Amherst, where
he is quite at home. The bluebird is sketched with like intent.

> Before you thought of Spring
> Except as a Surmise
> You see – God bless his suddenness –
> A Fellow in the Skies
> Of independent Hues
> A little weather worn
> Inspiriting habiliments
> Of Indigo and Brown –

With specimens of Song
As if for you to choose –
Discretion in the interval
With gay delays he goes
To some superior Tree
Without a single Leaf
And shouts for joy to Nobody
But his seraphic self –

The seven-quatrain poem that Emily Dickinson wrote in 1879 on the oriole may well have originated from Mrs. Jackson's suggestion. It has a splendor that imitation cannot reproduce. The oriole is "One of the ones that Midas touched," and a confiding prodigal:

A Pleader – a Dissembler –
An Epicure – a Thief –
Betimes an Oratorio –
An Ecstasy in chief –

He robs orchards and "cheats as he enchants."

The splendor of a Burmah
The Meteor of Birds,
Departing like a Pageant
Of Ballads and of Bards –

She is amused even by that pest, the rat, the concisest tenant, who pays no rent, a foe so reticent that no decree can prohibit him, who therefore exists as lawful "as Equilibrium." The frog is recalled by sound:

The long sigh of the Frog
Upon a Summer's Day
Enacts intoxication
Upon the Revery –
But his receding Swell
Substantiates a Peace
That makes the Ear inordinate
For corporal release –

It was Emily Dickinson's custom to enclose a note to friends, accompanied by a verse usually descriptive of the season or an aspect of nature. The flower poems were casually composed and seldom are distinctive. That on the arbutus is typical of the best.

> Pink – small – and punctual –
> Aromatic – low –
> Covert – in April –
> Candid – in May –
> Dear to the Moss –
> Known to the Knoll –
> Next to the Robin
> In every human Soul –
> Bold little Beauty
> Bedecked with thee
> Nature forswears
> Antiquity –

She selected the rose more often than any other flower to write about, but no poem on the subject is memorable. Though she many times attempted verse portraits of flowers, most seem unfinished or uninspired. The fact is that her special talent in nature verse lay in transmuting motion, and the evanescence of color in motion, into poetry, and flowers are still life. Her sensitivity to color, to yellow in particular, she acknowledged in one poem.

> Nature rarer uses Yellow
> Than another Hue.
> Saves she all of that for Sunsets
> Prodigal of Blue
>
> Spending Scarlet, like a Woman
> Yellow she affords
> Only scantly and selectly
> Like a Lover's Words.

It is perhaps more than coincidence that creatures touched with yellow — the oriole, the bee, the hummingbird, and the butterfly are the most convincingly delineated.

NATURE

A distinction can be made between the nature poems that are philosophical and those that are genre portraits. The former were written in the early sixties, when she was attempting explicitly to define her own relationships — to people, to the cosmos, to the unfathomable. Such are the poems "There's a certain Slant of Light," and "Further in Summer than the Birds," utterances which transmute moods of nature into profound reflection. But the best realized genre poems came later, when the turbulence created by her self-discoveries had subsided. It is true that she was trying her hand at such portraiture during the years of great productiveness, but the driving energy, which gave mystical beauty to poems concerned with abstract idea, overreached itself when she applied it to subjects calling for description only.

The point can be made clear by contrasting her two portraits of the hummingbird. The first she wrote about 1862. A poem in five quatrains, it is an attempt to suggest motion. She sees a vibration and hears a whir so rapid that only the stir of blossoms after the hummingbird's departure assures her of the truth of its presence. But the lines have been assembled laboriously and the figures remain awkward.

> Within my Garden, rides a Bird
> Upon a single Wheel –
> Whose spokes a dizzy Music make
> As 'twere a travelling Mill –
>
> He never stops, but slackens
> Above the Ripest Rose –
> Partakes without alighting
> And praises as he goes,
>
> Till every spice is tasted –
> And then his Fairy Gig
> Reels in remoter atmospheres –
> And I rejoin my Dog,
>
> And He and I, perplex us
> If positive, 'twere we –

Or bore the Garden in the Brain
This Curiosity –

But He, the best Logician,
Refers my clumsy eye –
To just vibrating Blossoms!
An Exquisite Reply!

The awkwardnesses are intrusive: the hummingbird praises, and
the rejoined dog is perplexed whether he too (or the poet?) saw
the bird. Emily Dickinson's skill in handling such themes she acquired much later. She never forgot what she wanted to express
about the hummingbird, as sound, iridescent color, vibration; as
instantaneous translation through space. Some eighteen years later
she returned to the theme, and in eight lines wrote a new poem
on the ubiquitous creature.

A Route of Evanescence
With a revolving Wheel –
A Resonance of Emerald –
A Rush of Cochineal –
And every Blossom on the Bush
Adjusts it's tumbled Head –
The mail from Tunis, probably,
An easy Morning's Ride –

The fulfillment of her art as a creator of the pageantry of nature
in motion she achieved in 1879, thereby adding abundantly to the
treasury of English verse.

IX

DEATH: *The White Exploit*

OTHER POETS OF COMPARABLE STATURE have made the theme of death central in much of their writing. Emily Dickinson did so in hers to an unusual degree. In one way or another she has drawn it into the texture of some five or six hundred poems. "All but Death," she wrote in 1863, "can be adjusted," and concludes:

> Death – unto itself exception –
> Is exempt from Change.

Much later in life she came to feel that "Maturity only enhances mystery, never decreases it." She viewed death from every possible angle, and left a record of her emotions and of her ideas about it in her poems. Death is a terror to be feared and shunned. It is a hideous, inequitable mistake; a trick played on trusting humanity by a sportive, insensate deity. It is a welcome relief from mortal ills. It is the blessed means to eternal happiness. But which of the attitudes is most valid, what assumptions about it are really true, she never decided.

The poems on death fall into three groups. There are those which are concerned with the physical demise of the body, some describing the act of dying with clinical detachment, some with emotional vehemence. Others muse upon death or depict the face and form of the body on which the gazer's attention is riveted. There are the poems in which death, the suitor, is personified — in which the theme deals less with life here and now, or of life to come, than with the precise moment of transition from one state to the other. And there are also the elegies and epitaphs — lyrical commemora-

tions of friends or of personages whom she has admired, like Elizabeth Barrett Browning or Charlotte Brontë.

There seems to be one persistent thought that binds together
this very large number of poems on death. It is the knowledge that
death snaps the lines of communication with those we have known
and loved, and creates the uncertainty in the minds of all mortals
whether that communication can ever be reëstablished. She gave
expression thus in 1864 to the basic human wonderment:

> Those who have been in the Grave the longest –
> Those who begin Today –
> Equally perish from our Practise –
> Death is the further way –
>
> Foot of the Bold did least attempt it –
> It – is the White Exploit –
> Once to achieve, annuls the power
> Once to communicate –

Death, whether occurring in the recesses of the past or in this instant of time, succeeds in accomplishing the one thing about which
she felt a gathering terror. Each such event left her irrecoverably
out of touch with those she had loved. "A Coffin – is a small Domain," she says in the same year,

> Yet able to contain
> A Rudiment of Paradise
> In it's diminished Plane.
>
> A Grave – is a restricted Breadth –
> Yet ampler than the Sun –
> And all the Seas He populates
> And Lands He looks upon
>
> To Him who on it's small Repose
> Bestows a single Friend –
> Circumference without Relief –
> Or Estimate – or End –

Such a terror can express itself in a variety of ways, and her poems were not only the means by which she relieved her apprehensions, but the medium through which she adjusted herself to the necessity and to the pleasure of living and being richly alive.

Emily Dickinson's earliest intimate experience of death came in April 1844, when she was thirteen. Sophia Holland (not a member of the J. G. Holland family), the fifteen-year-old daughter of a neighbor, was stricken fatally. The somewhat younger Emily witnessed the death of the girl whom she evidently greatly admired. Two years later the shattering impression which the circumstance had left with her was so vivid that she recorded it in detail in a letter to Abiah Root.

I have never lost but one friend near my age & with whom my thoughts & her own were the same. It was before you came to Amherst. My friend was Sophia Holland . . . I visited her often in sickness & watched over her bed. But at length Reason fled and the physician forbid any but the nurse to go into her room. Then it seemed to me I should die too if I could not be permitted to watch over her or even to look at her face. At length the doctor said she must die & allowed me to look at her a moment through the open door. I took off my shoes and stole softly to the sick room. There she lay mild and beautiful as in health & her pale features lit up with an unearthly smile. I looked as long as friends would permit & when they told me I must look no longer I let them lead me away. I shed no tear, for my heart was too full to weep, but after she was laid in her coffin & I felt I could not call her back again I gave way to a fixed melancholy. I told no one the cause of my grief, though it was gnawing at my very heart strings. I was not well & I went to Boston & stayed a month & my health improved so that my spirits were better.

Patently the child needed to be out of Amherst, and the parents arranged that their overwrought daughter spend the month of May with relatives in Cambridge and Boston. Emily of course was too young to realize why she had insisted on staying in the sickroom "as long as friends would permit." She had done so partly through a normal curiosity about the physical incident of death. But one also feels that for this oddly sensitive child the impulse welled more deeply; that it came from her precocious knowledge that death establishes new perspectives for the living, and that the experience of such sensations can be most acutely registered in the presence of death.

Six years later, when she was twenty-one, she describes in a letter to Jane Humphrey how her imagination has led her to pretend that she sees herself in her own coffin. To some extent she is daring herself to the emotional indulgence because, as William Hazlitt once put it: "No young man believes he shall ever die"; and as she herself later expressed the idea: "Ourselves we do inter with sweet derision."

Your home is broken, Jennie; my home is whole; that makes a sad, sad difference, and when I think of it more, it don't seem strange to me, as it did at first, that you could leave it . . . It doesn't seem one bit as if my friends would die, for I do love them so, that even should death come after them, it don't seem as if they'd go; yet there's Abbie and Mr. Humphrey, and Mary and many a dear one, whom I love just as dearly, and they are not upon earth this lovely Sabbath evening. Bye and bye, we'll all be gone, Jennie, does it seem as if we would? The other day I tried to think how I should look with my eyes shut, and a little white gown on, and a snowdrop on my breast, and I fancied I heard the neighbors stealing in so softly, to look down in my face – so fast asleep – so still, Oh, Jennie, will you and I really become like this?
Don't mind what I say, darling, I'm a naughty bad girl, to say sad things, and make you cry out. I think of the grave very often, and how much it has got of mine, and whether I can ever stop it from carrying off what I love; that makes me sometimes speak of it, when I don't intend.

For us, though one doubts if for Jane, the sentimentality is oppressive; but the thought was prompted by a sensitivity to and possessiveness about friends which, as Emily Dickinson felt in 1852 when she wrote Jane, and incessantly thereafter, death always betrayed.

From first to last her concern with death was neither morbid nor idle. It was on occasion clinical in the same way and for the same reasons that Jonathan Edwards observed and reported on the workings on the "soul's affections." It is clinical in the way a medical examiner hopes to test the validity of a theory and submits himself first to the test, or watches a patient with alert sensibilities to detect the true symptoms and eliminate the false.

Emily Dickinson early undertook to discover whether as a poet she could record the mystery of death, and she asked the obvious questions. Do those about to die experience some occult sensation, some portentous vision which they can communicate? Can they convey or seek to convey a new mode of sensation to the living? Does physical contemplation of the dead, engaged in to give the beholder a new detachment and new frames of reference, lead perhaps even to a fleeting glimpse past the bourn from which no traveler returns? "All this and more, though *is* there more? More than Love and Death?" She had always asked these questions, as Mrs. Holland had long since known, and understood. "Then tell me it's name!" She herself never really understood that she had answered her question by the act of creating her poems.

It is easier to answer such a question if somewhere in one's career those we love can give assurance that the way of life we choose is valid. Nobody could do that for Emily Dickinson, for she had chosen to keep her poetry in large part from the world. She had elected to be a poet without recognition or fame in her lifetime, but much that she writes about life and death must be read with an understanding that she "lived" in writing it and "died" because it was imperfectly shared. Friendship and love fulfill themselves through the creations of the mind as well as of the body, of the body as well as of the mind. She was equally dedicated to children and poetry. It was destined that she create only poetry.

The earliest poems concerning death and moments of dying are sentimentally funereal, like "There's something quieter than sleep/ Within this inner room," "Taken from men this morning/ Carried by men today," or "Delayed till she had ceased to know," and "Going to Heaven/ I dont know when." The inspiration for them did not well up from inner springs, and in one instance at least it derived from a book illustration. "A poor, torn heart – a tattered heart," rescued by angels who "carried it to God," survives in a copy onto which Emily stitched two pictures clipped from her father's copy of *The Old Curiosity Shop*. The lines were inspired by Little Nell's weeping grandfather.

There is a depressingly large number of such verses in the packets of 1858 and 1859. "If I should die" is rescued from complete bathos by the kind of whimsy for which too often, one fears, she had been commended.

> If I should die,
> And you should live –
> And time should gurgle on . . .
>
> Tis sweet to know that stocks will stand
> When we with Daisies lie . . .

Yet within the space of two years she bridged an immense gulf.

Her musings in a graveyard she wrought with eloquence in "Safe in their Alabaster Chambers." The theme of her poems on death may be the difference in the interests of those no longer concerned with the issues of existence, as in "What care the Dead, for Chanticleer," or it may be the distance of the dead from the living, as in "Under the Light, yet under." The eight-stanza verse "Who occupies this House" ponders the identity of the dwellers in the city of the dead. She speculates that the place was unknown:

> Until a Pioneer, as
> Settlers often do
> Liking the quiet of the Place
> Attracted more unto –
>
> And from a Settlement
> A Capitol has grown
> Distinguished for the gravity
> Of every Citizen

Any death for Emily Dickinson was an experience which she too shared, and the death of friends was one in which she emotionally participated. She witnessed it from two directions: through the eyes of the observer, and by construction through the sensations of the dying. This compound vision she embodies in such poems as "No Notice gave she, but a Change," and " 'Twas Crisis – All the length had passed." The quiet irony of "To die takes just a little while" is characteristic of Dickinson's poetry, and here the images flash with sharp precision.

> The Dying need but little, Dear,
> A Glass of Water's all,
> A Flower's unobtrusive Face
> To punctuate the Wall,
>
> A Fan, perhaps, a Friend's Regret
> And Certainty that one
> No color in the Rainbow
> Perceive, when you are gone.

"How many times these low feet staggered" is written from the point of view of one who stands alone in a room gazing at a dead body. Intimate touches associate the deceased with her homely labors. One cannot move the "adamantine fingers" which will never again wear a thimble. Dull flies buzz, the sun shines bravely through the "freckled pane," and a cobweb now swings "fearless" from the ceiling. In "I've seen a Dying Eye," she describes the search of the dying one for something just before the sight is obscured by death:

> Then Cloudier become –
> And then – obscure with Fog –
> And then – be soldered down
> Without disclosing what it be
> 'Twere blessed to have seen –

The search, it is clear, is in fact being made by the poet who, in the presence of death, hopes to find an answer to the riddle of death. It belongs to the same order of poems as " 'Tis so appalling it exhilirates," in which she concludes that

> Looking at Death, is Dying –
> Just let go the Breath –
> And not the pillow at your Cheek
> So Slumbereth –
>
> Others, Can wrestle –
> Your's, is done –
> And so of Wo, bleak dreaded – come,
> It sets the Fright at liberty –
> And Terror's free –
> Gay, Ghastly, Holiday!

The moment of death or the reflections during the hour following it were especially impressive. "This that would greet – an hour ago –/ Is quaintest Distance – now," she muses:

> Match me the Silver Reticence –
> Match me the Solid Calm –

In "These saw Visions" the eyes, cheeks, hair, mouth, and feet of the deceased are scanned, and the fingers especially:

> These – we held among our own –
> Fingers of the Slim Aurora –
> Not so arrogant – this Noon –

She pleads, in "The World – feels dusty/ When we stop to Die," for some share in the moment of death of another:

> Mine be the Ministry
> When thy Thirst comes –
> Dews of Thessaly, to fetch –
> And Hybla Balms –

The intensity of her gaze is matched on occasion by an impersonality which is forced upon her by the realization that the body is now but a husk.

> Too cold is this
> To warm with Sun –
> Too stiff to bended be –

> To joint the Agate were a work –
> Outstaring Masonry –
>
> How went the Agile Kernel out
> Contusion of the Husk
> Nor Rip, nor wrinkle indicate
> But just an Asterisk.

The morbidity may repel the reader as perhaps it did the writer, since the poem did not go beyond the worksheet stage. But the state of mind is integral with the process of viewing death in all possible ways in order to make final adjustment to it. In 1861 she seems to have written "A Clock stopped" with similar intent, and also at some remove. The moment of death, when the heart ceases to beat, is metaphorically described in the first stanza.

> A Clock stopped –
> Not the Mantel's –
> Geneva's farthest skill
> Cant put the puppet bowing –
> That just now dangled still –

By now no physician's skill can restore life. The second stanza goes back to the moment before death when the dying person, hunched with pain, realizes the awful moment is at hand and, at the final stroke of noon, succumbs.

> An awe came on the Trinket!
> The Figures hunched, with pain –
> Then quivered out of Decimals –
> Into Degreeless Noon –

The scene described is so entirely metaphorical that one suspects she is imagining the moment of her own death. Certainly she is not realistically observing that of a friend. She projects a situation which concerns a person whom those who have some claim to love (the shopman, for instance) are powerless to help. Time thenceforth must be reckoned by "Decades of Arrogance." That which cannot be repaired is indeed a trinket.

It will not stir for Doctor's –
This Pendulum of snow –
The Shopman importunes it –
While cool – concernless No –

Nods from the Gilded pointers –
Nods from the Seconds slim –
Decades of Arrogance between
The Dial life –
And Him –

The superb poem "I felt a funeral in my brain" fulfills its intent of evoking the characteristic mood of New England funerals and their appalling effect upon a person both sensitive, and acutely allergic, to them. The mourners keep "treading – treading" until they are seated, and then the service like a drum keeps "beating – beating," until the poet's mind seems numb. The sense of desolation, and the Poe-like effect of the maelstrom created by the whole procedure, are focused with extraordinary skill in the three concluding stanzas.

And then I heard them lift a Box
And creak across my Soul
With those same Boots of Lead, again,
Then Space -- began to toll,

As All the Heavens were a Bell,
And Being, but an Ear,
And I, and Silence, some strange Race
Wrecked, solitary, here –

And then a Plank in Reason, broke,
And I dropped down, and down –
And hit a World, at every plunge,
And Finished knowing – then –

The six-stanza poem "There's been a Death in the Opposite House" is an unforgettably vivid reconstruction of a child's memory of a death impersonally witnessed from the outside of the neighbor's house in which the death occurred.

DEATH

The Neighbors rustle in and out –
The Doctor – drives away –
A Window opens like a Pod –
Abrupt – mechanically –

A mattress is aired, children hurry by, the minister arrives "as if the house were his," followed by the milliner and "the man of the Appalling Trade."

There'll be that Dark Parade –

Of Tassells – and of Coaches – soon –
It's easy as a Sign –
The Intuition of the News –
In just a Country Town –

The technical perfection of the four-stanza poem "She lay as if at play" can be felt in the brevity and delicate restraint conveyed by language so concrete that the reader feels almost a shock of surprise to realize that the poem in point of fact describes, not the death, but the corpse of a dead child.

Her merry Arms, half dropt –
As if for lull of sport –
An instant had forgot
The Trick to start –

Her dancing Eyes – ajar –
As if their Owner were
Still sparkling through
For fun – at you –

Equally remarkable for its virtuosity, "I heard a Fly buzz – when I died," belongs to a somewhat different order among the lyrics which ponder the crises of sorrow. It appears to have been written in 1862. With that combination of condensed precision and eloquence which give her best poems their rank, she transmits the sensations which she imagines she might feel during the last moments before death. The bereaved family at the bedside are past the point of tears, for the moment of death has arrived.

> And Breaths were gathering firm
> For that last Onset – when the King
> Be witnessed – in the Room –

A stillness such as that "between the heaves of storm" prepares the reader physically to hear the final agonizing gasp of the dying. The buzzing fly, so familiar a part of the natural order of persistent household discomforts, is brought in at the last to give the touch of petty irritabilities that are concomitant with living – and indeed – with dying.

> With Blue – uncertain stumbling Buzz –
> Between the light – and me –
> And then the Windows failed – and then
> I could not – see to see –

It is of course because Emily Dickinson had from childhood felt an unusual sensitivity about such events that she is here uniquely able to give reality to the moment.

A friend of Henry James, as the story is told, on learning that James had attended a funeral in the home of a family where James was not on speaking terms, asked why he had done so. James replied: "Where emotion is, there am I." It is a remark that Emily Dickinson could have made. "The last Night that she lived" needs no further documentation than the poem itself to witness her presence in the room of the dying. The evidence of the packet into which she transcribed it suggests that she wrote it in 1866. It happens that on May third of that year, Laura Dickey, the young wife of Frank W. Dickey of Michigan, and a daughter of L. M. Hills of Amherst, died at her parents' home. The Hills were lifelong neighbors of the Dickinsons, and their property adjoined the Dickinsons' on the east. Emily Dickinson may or may not have been present at the time of Laura Dickey's death. There is no record that she was, but knowing the neighborly relationship of the Hills and the Dickinsons, and Emily's natural impulses, she may have been. Laura Dickey's death is the only one in Amherst that year in the household of friends or neighbors that has the same probability of documentation.

Whatever the source of inspiration, Emily Dickinson in this poem takes the reader with her into the presence of the dying. The stanzas have the same combination of restrained emotion and homely, concrete detail as Dante Gabriel Rossetti's "My Sister's Sleep," but the poem goes further in its effort toward adjustment to the final mystery. There is envy (Jealousy) of the discovery that the dying one will make, and a resentment (Blame) that God has failed to make mortals privy to the great secret.

> The last Night that She lived
> It was a common Night
> Except the Dying – this to Us
> Made Nature different
>
> We noticed smallest things –
> Things overlooked before
> By this great light upon our Minds
> Italicized – as 'twere.
>
> As We went out and in
> Between Her final Room
> And Rooms where Those to be alive
> Tomorrow were, a Blame
>
> That Others could exist
> While She must finish quite
> A Jealousy for Her arose
> So nearly infinite –
>
> We waited while She passed –
> It was a narrow time –
> Too jostled were Our Souls to speak
> At length the Notice came.
>
> She mentioned, and forgot –
> Then lightly as a Reed
> Bent to the Water, struggled scarce –
> Consented, and was dead –

And We – We placed the Hair –
And drew the Head erect –
And then an awful leisure was
Belief to regulate –

Among the many poems that recollect the loved dead are those
that search for the imponderable, as for instance "What did They
do since I saw Them?" Here the poet yearns to see and touch them
again, to learn whether they are occupied or homesick. In one of
the best realized of her graveyard musings she goes so far as to
suggest that death may be a fulfillment:

This quiet Dust was Gentlemen and Ladies
And Lads and Girls –
Was laughter and ability and Sighing
And Frocks and Curls.

This Passive Place a Summer's nimble mansion
Where Bloom and Bees
Exist an Oriental Circuit
Then cease, like these –

On a rare June day her happiness in existing expresses itself by
a thought first for those who once lived but now do not. Do the
dead wish they were again mortal and alive? She begins with the
thought "I'm sorry for the Dead – Today." She feels

A Trouble lest they're homesick –
Those Farmers – and their Wives –
Set separate from the Farming –
And all the Neighbor's lives –

A Wonder if the Sepulchre
Dont feel a lonesome way –
When Men – and Boys – and Carts – and June,
Go down the Fields to "Hay" –

Two love poems written in 1862 compel attention here by their
macabre vehemence. Since the lover is unobtainable in life, the poet

asks for his body after death. The one beginning "If I may have it when it's dead/ I'll be contented – so" concludes:

> Forgive me, if to stroke thy frost
> Out visions Paradise!

"Promise this – when you be Dying" asks the privilege of being summoned when the lover dies, and of laying out his body. "Mine belong your latest sighing/ Mine to Belt your Eye," she says, not with a coin but with her lips. The poems offer a glimpse into the psychological adjustment Emily Dickinson was having to make in that year. Both were left in semifinal drafts, so rough as to suggest that she could not finish them.

A quite different order of poems are those which personify Death, a nebulous creature at first, who soon develops the stature of a true character of fiction. "One dignity delays for all," written in 1859, pictures Death as a potentate, almost oriental in the absoluteness of his sway and the splendor of his court. His colors are purple, and thus doubly associated: with royalty and with the color of the ample bow of ribbons attached at the time of death to the front door of New England houses. The "dignity" which none can avoid includes, besides the purple, a coach, footmen, a chamber, and a state gathering. There will be bells too for the processional march, with solemn service and a hundred raised hats. This pomp, surpassing ermine, death prepares:

> When simple you, and I,
> Present our meek escutcheon
> And claim the rank to die!

Exactly the same ceremony of investiture is described in the slightly later poem "Wait till the majesty of Death/ Invests so mean a brow," where "this democrat," dressed in "everlasting robes," receives the homage of "obsequious angels." Twice again (in 1862) he is the despot. Here too as earlier in "I heard a Fly buzz when I died," we wait "For that last Onset – when the King/ Be witnessed – in the Room." But in "Triumph may be of several kinds" Death, that "Old Imperator," has been met and vanquished by his adversary Faith. This is the last poem in which Emily Dickinson imagines death as a swollen tyrant. She now returns the morality puppet to its box because she already has created one of the most extraordinary characters in American literature.

With few exceptions characters that gain dimension and live in the heart and memory of succeeding generations do so by virtue of their solid reality. It may well be that at the end the author, who has envisioned them as universal creatures, endows them with symbolic meaning, and lets them withdraw from the stage in a manner that suggests his deepened intent. King Henry's contemptuous banishment of Falstaff to prison does more than dismiss the aging knight and conclude his career. It is Shakespeare's way of saying that we must always allow for the possibility that a friend in office is a friend lost. Colonel Newcome on his deathbed, answering "adsum" to an imagined roll call on the threshold of the new life, as he had been taught to answer on the threshold of the life now completed, links all futures with all pasts. Leatherstocking appears in many names and guises, but Cooper, ready to let him depart full of years and forest wisdom, returns him to the world of nature as a myth and a symbol of the prairie and the vanishing woods. Readers of *Moby-Dick* discover long before the end that Ahab is a force of nature as well as the tormented captain of a whaling ship. Huckleberry Finn will never grow older, because Mark Twain conferred immortal youth upon him by the simple expedient of having Huck remark at the end of the story that he is lighting out for the territory ahead of the rest, lest Aunt Sally adopt and civilize him.

Emily Dickinson personified Death, but her method of doing so reverses the usual procedure. She started with a symbol which she altered into a reality. The method is inherently necessary when the symbol is personified, but there are few writers who, experiencing such a symbol intensely, have the artist's endowment whereby the substance is made flesh. In respect to that ability, as in other ways already noted, she calls to mind William Blake who, like her, began with a symbol which demanded from the artist a concrete form. Thus Death as Emily Dickinson conceived and delineated him is a protean figure, part element of nature, part erlking, part Grendel, but mostly country squire: a suave, elusive, persuasive, insinuating character, but always a very genteel and attentive Amherst friend and suitor. It is the person whom she described to Mrs. Holland in 1865. Sue's sister Martha Gilbert Smith, who had previously lost a child, was stricken a second time by the death of her two-year-old daughter. Emily wrote that Sue "is still with the sister who put her child in an ice nest last Monday forenoon. The redoubtable God! I notice when Death has been introduced, he frequently calls, making it desirable to forestall his advances."

In 1859 there is a dim suggestion of him in " 'Goodnight,' because we must," where he is represented as a saucy seraph whom she tries to cajole into revealing his mysteries to her, appealing in the end to her (heavenly) father, as a child being teased past endurance might do. But Death really first becomes dimensional in the following year in "Dust is the only secret." He is identified as a neighbor's boy who has grown up in Amherst and who, because everybody has vaguely known him, is now somewhat legendary. He is:

> . . . the only one
> You cannot find out all about
> In his native town –
>
> Nobody knew his Father –
> Never was a Boy –
> Had'nt any playmates
> Nor "Early history" –

The biographical sketch now becomes more indistinct, fading into snatches of local gossip:

> Industrious – Laconic –
> Punctual – Sedate –
> Bolder than a Brigand –
> Swifter than a Fleet –

Builds like a Bird – too –
Christ robs the nest –
Robin after Robin
Smuggled to rest –

At the end he has metamorphosed into a father robin who, having turned suddenly into a smuggler, acts as agent for a divine robber baron. In "The only Ghost I ever saw" the personification is likewise both concrete and abstract. Death is a person and also a force of nature. He wears a lacy garment and moves with silent, rapid gait. Shy in her presence, he politely engages her in a "transient" interview. Recalling his elusiveness and the sound of his diminishing laughter, she is in the mood to say: "And God forbid I look behind/ Since that Appalling Day."

It is the well-bred gentility of Death, who takes on the nature of a cavalier suitor, that distinguishes him in several poems written in 1862. He woos with gifts in "For Death – or rather," offering "Room, Escape from Circumstances, and a Name." But the entreated one remains perplexed, not knowing how to compare Death's gifts with Life's, since the equivalent of Life's values cannot be known until we die. The bold impetuosity of the suitor, this time a John Alden in the service of God, is conveyed by the meter as well as the thought in the two stanzas beginning:

It's Coming – the postponeless Creature –
It gains the Block – and now – it gains the Door –
Chooses it's latch – from all the other fastenings –
Enters – with a "You know Me – Sir?"

The setting for "I read my sentence – steadily" might be Main Street in Amherst on any summer day. The poet informs her soul of the approaching extremity.

But she, and Death, acquainted –
Meet tranquilly, as friends –
Salute, and pass, without a Hint –
And there, the Matter ends –

The rival claims of an earthly lover and of Death are visioned in "I live with Him – I see His Face," for Death alone can forestall her choice and prevent marriage:

> And that – by Right that He
> Presents a Claim invisible –
> No Wedlock – granted Me –

In "Death is a supple suitor," written some twelve years later, Death still woos stealthily by "pallid innuendoes and dim approach"; and he carries his intended bride to a troth and to unknown kindred who are as "responsive as porcelain." On some occasions he is a genteel householder whose rooms are made habitable by pale furniture and metallic peace. Sometimes he holds debate with the spirit. "Death is a Dialogue between/ The Spirit and the Dust," she says, in which the spirit, not deigning to pursue the argument, turns away after laying off for evidence of the encounter "An Overcoat of Clay." He is also a despoiler, a Grendel to be hunted to his ravine or chased to his den.

> The Frost of Death was on the Pane –
> "Secure your Flower" said he.
> Like Sailors fighting with a Leak
> We fought Mortality.
>
> Our passive Flower we held to Sea –
> To Mountain – To the Sun –
> Yet even on his Scarlet Shelf
> To crawl the Frost begun –
>
> We pried him back
> Ourselves we wedged
> Himself and her between,
> Yet easy as a narrow Snake
> He forked his way along
>
> Till all her helpless beauty bent
> And then our wrath begun –
> We hunted him to his Ravine
> We chased him to his Den –

> We hated Death and hated Life
> And nowhere was to go –
> Than Sea and continent there is
> A larger – it is Woe

He is the grave itself in "Bereaved of all, I went abroad," where she finds that Death has preceded her, and occupied her lodgings and her bed. She tries to lose him in the crowd or in the sea, but she cannot shake him. She makes a final effort:

> In Cups of artificial Drowse
> To steep it's shape away –
> The Grave – was finished – but the spade
> Remained in Memory –

In 1863 Death came into full stature as a person. "Because I could not stop for Death" is a superlative achievement wherein Death becomes one of the great characters of literature.

It is almost impossible in any critique to define exactly the kind of reality which her character Death attains, simply because the protean shifts of form are intended to forestall definition. A poem can convey the nuances of exultation, agony, compassion, or any mystical mood. But no one can successfully define mysticism because the logic of language has no place for it. One must therefore assume that the reality of Death, as Emily Dickinson conceived him, is to be perceived by the reader in the poems themselves. Any analysis can do no more than suggest what may be looked for.

In "Because I could not stop for Death" Emily Dickinson envisions Death as a person she knew and trusted, or believed that she could trust. He might be any Amherst gentleman, a William Howland or an Elbridge Bowdoin, or any of the coming lawyers or teachers or ministers whom she remembered from her youth, with whom she had exchanged valentines, and who at one time or another had acted as her squire.

> Because I could not stop for Death –
> He kindly stopped for me –

DEATH

> The Carriage held but just Ourselves –
> And Immortality.

The carriage holds but the two of them, yet the ride, as she states with quiet emphasis, is a last ride together. Clearly there has been no deception on his part. They drive in a leisurely manner, and she feels completely at ease. Since she understands it to be a last ride, she of course expects it to be unhurried. Indeed, his graciousness in taking time to stop for her at that point and on that day in her life when she was so busy she could not possibly have taken time to stop for him, is a mark of special politeness. She is therefore quite willing to put aside her work. And again, since it is to be her last ride, she can dispense with her spare moments as well as her active ones.

> We slowly drove – He knew no haste
> And I had put away
> My labor and my leisure too
> For His Civility –

She notes the daily routine of the life she is passing from. Children playing games during a school recess catch her eye at the last. And now the sense of motion is quickened. Or perhaps more exactly one should say that the sense of time comes to an end as they pass the cycles of the day and the seasons of the year, at a period of both ripeness and decline.

> We passed the School, where Children strove
> At Recess – in the Ring –
> We passed the Fields of Gazing Grain –
> We passed the Setting Sun –

How insistently "passed" echoes through the stanza! She now conveys her feeling of being outside time and change, for she corrects herself to say that the sun passed them, as it of course does all who are in the grave. She is aware of dampness and cold, and becomes suddenly conscious of the sheerness of the dress and scarf which she now discovers that she wears.

Or rather – He passed Us –
The Dews drew quivering and chill –
For only Gossamer, my Gown –
My Tippet – only Tulle –

The two concluding stanzas, with progressively decreasing concreteness, hasten the final identification of her "House." It is the
slightly rounded surface "of the Ground," with a scarcely visible
roof and a cornice "in the Ground." To time and seasonal change,
which have already ceased, is now added motion. Cessation of all
activity and creativeness is absolute. At the end, in a final instantaneous flash of memory, she recalls the last objects before her eyes
during the journey: the heads of the horses that bore her, as she
had surmised they were doing from the beginning, toward – it is
the last word – "Eternity."

We paused before a House that seemed
A Swelling of the Ground –
The Roof was scarcely visible –
The Cornice – in the Ground –

Since then – 'tis Centuries – and yet
Feels shorter than the Day
I first surmised the Horses Heads
Were toward Eternity –

Gradually, too, one realizes that Death as a person has receded into
the background, mentioned last only impersonally in the opening
words "We paused" of the fifth stanza, where his services as squire
and companion are over. In this poem concrete realism melds into
"awe and circumference" with matchless economy.

The elegies that Emily Dickinson wrote as tributes to the memory of persons she had loved range in quality from the least to the
finest of her creations. Many are intended for clearly identifiable
people, but a large portion of them is so generalized or so indefinite
that readers are unlikely ever to know whether the verses were
intended for any actual person. Most of such poems were written

early and include "Her sweet turn to leave the homestead," "He gave away his life," "Ambition cannot find him," and "Taken from men this morning."

The greater number of the commemorative poems were sent to friends on the occasion of a bereavement. When her mother's favorite sister Lavinia Norcross died in Boston in April 1860, Emily sent an eight-line verse to the motherless teen-age cousins Louise and Frances. It is pedestrian and commonplace, but the stricken children would accept it as appropriate.

> Mama never forgets her birds,
> Though in another tree,
> She looks down just as often
> And just as tenderly
> As when her little mortal nest
> With cunning care she wove –
> If either of her "sparrows fall",
> She "notices," above.

Early also is the poem written in memory of Charlotte Brontë, which leaves scant impact on the reader. Brontë is a bird here also, whose cage, "All overgrown by cunning moss," is laid away because the bird has flown to other latitudes.

> Oh what an afternoon for Heaven,
> When "Bronte" entered there!

Emily Dickinson says she was first awakened to the immediacy of poetry by reading the poems of Elizabeth Barrett Browning, and she wrote three in memory of the "Anglo-Florentine."

> I think I was enchanted
> When first a little Girl –
> I read that Foreign Lady –

The occasion was such that "The Days to Mighty Metres stept."

> I could not have defined the change –
> Conversion of the Mind

> Like Sanctifying in the Soul
> Is witnessed – not explained

Her great admiration she again expressed as a personal loss in the poem that says: "I went to thank Her/ But She slept," concluding:

> 'Twas Short – to cross the Sea –
> To look upon Her like – alive –
> But turning back – 'twas slow –

Most of the elegies she wrote in later years. Even when they memorialize no occasion significant to the recipient, she sent them to friends if she believed their quality gave her warrant for doing so. Such is the nature of one she sent to Colonel Higginson in 1871.

> Step lightly on this narrow spot –
> The broadest Land that grows
> Is not so ample as the Breast
> These Emerald Seams enclose.
>
> Step lofty, for this name be told
> As far as Cannon dwell
> Or Flag subsist or Fame export
> Her deathless Syllable.

But generally those which she sent to friends were written for special occasions. When news came that Joseph Sweetser, her aunt Catherine's husband, had walked out of his New York house one day in 1874, never to be heard of again, she wrote a letter to her aunt, of whom she was very fond, incorporating lines that were personally felt.

> Death's Waylaying not the sharpest
> Of the thefts of Time –
> There Marauds a sorer Robber,
> Silence – is his Name –
> No Assault, nor any Menace
> Doth betoken him.
> But from Life's consummate Cluster –
> He supplants the Balm.

Her father's death on 16 June 1874 fixed that date in her memory and was the occasion for several elegies. In the January following she wrote this unforgettable sentence in a letter to Mrs. Holland: "Mother is asleep in the Library – Vinnie – in the Dining Room – Father – in the Masked Bed – in the Marl House." She follows it with a quatrain.

> How soft his Prison is –
> How sweet those sullen Bars –
> No Despot – but the King of Down
> Invented that Repose!

On the first anniversary, in June 1875, she wrote Samuel Bowles: "The paper wanders so I cannot write my name on it, so I give you father's portrait instead." Then follow these lines:

> As Summer into Autumn slips
> And yet we sooner say
> The Summer than the Autumn – lest
> We turn the sun away
>
> And count it almost an affront
> The Presence to concede
> Of one however lovely – not
> The one that we have loved
>
> So we evade the charge of Years
> On one attempting shy
> The Circumvention of the shaft
> Of Life's Declivity.

By March 1876 she would write Colonel Higginson at greater emotional remove:

When I think of my Father's lonely Life and lonelier Death, there is this redress –

> Take all away –
> The only thing worth larceny
> Is left – the Immortality –

But the finest elegiac utterance about her father she made still later. In mid-June 1877 she wrote the Colonel in a pensive mood. "Since my Father's dying – everything sacred enlarges so – it was dim to own." She speculates about immortality, and leads into the following quatrain by saying: "I was rereading your 'Decoration.' You may have forgotten it."

> Lay this Laurel on the One
> Too intrinsic for Renown –
> Laurel – vail your deathless tree –
> Him you chasten, that is He!

Few poets in the language have achieved fulfillment by way of the single quatrain with greater sureness than Emily Dickinson. The immediate source of her inspiration for the lines was a seven-stanza Civil War elegy that Higginson had contributed to *Scribner's Monthly* in the same month and year that her father died. The association had prompted the rereading, and her own poem. Years later Higginson made a copy of it for Mrs. Todd at the time they were preparing copy for the second volume of *Poems*. "I copy for the pleasure of copying it," he said, "though you may have it," and creditably adds: "She wrote it after re-reading my 'Decoration.' It is the condensed essence of that & so far finer." But Higginson never knew, so delicately had Emily Dickinson hinted at it, that the elegy she wrote and sent to him was her way of paying respects to the memory of her father.

The year 1882 brought the deaths of the Reverend Charles Wadsworth and Emily's mother. The event of Wadsworth's death gave her occasion to write at least one poem.

> Obtaining but our own Extent
> In whatsoever Realm –
> 'Twas Christ's own personal Expanse
> That bore him from the Tomb –

To Maria Whitney she wrote that the grief of wonder at her mother's fate "made the winter short, and each night I reach finds my lungs more breathless, seeking what it means." The thought is followed by the two six-line stanzas beginning: "To the bright east she flies."

The grief she felt after the death of her nephew Gilbert in 1883 she expressed in notes to Sue. In the course of one she reminds her sister: "Hopelessness in it's first Film has not leave to last." She concludes the letter with the elegy "Expanse cannot be lost," which ends:

> Escape more slowly
> To thy Tracts of Sheen –
> The Tent is listening,
> But the Troops are gone!

One of the elegies for Gilbert, Sue never released for publication, but kept among her private papers.

> The Heart has many Doors –
> I can but knock
> For any sweet "Come in"
> Impelled to hark –
> Not saddened by repulse,
> Repast to me
> That somewhere, there exists,
> Supremacy –

Five lines which she sent to Sue at the time shed light on her concept of death and the hereafter, and it bears out in a striking way what has been apparent from the beginning, although sometimes only implicitly.

> Immured in Heaven!
> What a Cell!
> Let every Bondage be,
> Thou sweetest of the Universe,
> Like that which ravished thee!

Her identification of Heaven as a "cell" in which Gilbert is immured (entombed or imprisoned) and in bondage is unusual. She has here also given the word an extension of meaning. Heaven clearly is desirable, because the poet wishes every bondage, every sweetness thus ravaged, to be like his. The sweetness of honey which the bee gains by ravaging a flower — a trope which she repeatedly employs in her poems — is also entombed in a cell whose form and shape bear noticeable likeness to a small coffin. "Let every enslavement be as desirable as that of yours, which furnishes delight to the divine appropriator, even though it is gained by depredation." To the last she clung to her thought that "Christ robs the nest," although she acknowledges that such theft results in a bondage that is welcome and desirable.

There remained two further distressing bereavements to be faced. Judge Lord died at Salem in March 1884. She composed three elegies in his memory: "Go thy great way," "Though the great Waters sleep," and "Quite empty, quite at rest." She told Mrs. Holland of his death in a letter that begins: "When I tell my sweet Mrs Holland that I have lost another friend, she will not wonder I do not write, but that I raise my Heart to a drooping syllable." Then she adds:

> Quite empty, quite at rest,
> The Robin locks her Nest, and tries her Wings.
> She does not know a Route
> But puts her Craft about
>   For *rumored* Springs.
> She does not ask for Noon —
> She does not ask for Boon,
> Crumbless and homeless, of but one request —
>   The Birds she lost.

It is unusual among elegies, for the poet speaks throughout solely about herself. The bird who stays watches her nest slowly depleted as her brood vanishes one by one. It is a song lamenting the impoverishment, to the point of bankruptcy, of the bereft.

One of her very last poems — and by now she composed only elegies — was incorporated in the spring of 1886 in a letter to

Colonel Higginson, sent to him but a short time before her own death. She thanks him for a copy of the sonnet he had composed in memory of Helen Jackson, and adds:

> The immortality she gave
> We borrowed at her Grave –
> For just one Plaudit famishing,
> The Might of Human love –

At the end the songs are inspired by death, but the theme is the might of human love.

THE COLOSSAL SUBSTANCE
OF IMMORTALITY

FOR EMILY DICKINSON the themes of death and immortality were, quite properly, two distinct subjects. She wrote a very large number of poems on death, more in fact than she did upon the theme of immortality. Yet with the latter subject she worked out a philosophic testament as profound as it is daring. By 1862 her new, if delayed, maturity led her to a vision of "the Colossal substance of Immortality."

> The Soul's Superior instants
> Occur to Her – alone –
> When friend – and Earth's occasion
> Have infinite withdrawn –
>
> Or She – Herself – ascended
> To too remote a Hight
> For lower Recognition
> Than Her Omnipotent –
>
> This Mortal Abolition
> Is seldom – but as fair
> As Apparition – subject
> To Autocratic Air –
>
> Eternity's disclosure
> To favorites – a few –
> Of the Colossal substance
> Of Immortality

Like Browning, she would hate that death bandaged her eyes, and she looked upon the mystery of the unknowable with all her faculties alert. "You mention Immortality," she once commented in a letter to Higginson; "That is the Flood subject." Her discoveries about the human heart were made, as they always must be, through travail and bitter self-appraisal. "To learn the Transport by the Pain," as she expressed it in 1860, "This is the Sovreign Anguish!" Most of her thoughts on the all-engrossing subject of the meaning of meaning she expressed in poetry written during the span of three or four years, before she was thirty-five years old.

The two intellectual and spiritual forces that shaped her thinking were the Puritan traditions into which she was born, and the romantic and transcendental doctrines that were general in the New England of her youth. New England transcendentalism emphasized the view that sense experiences are fundamental in reality, and asserted the primacy of spiritual over material values. In common with Puritanism it was pervasively ethical, but it differed from the older orthodoxy by repudiating traditional authority and by sharing with the Quakers a belief that man's inner nature is unique and that therefore men must follow their intuitions, each man by way of his own "inner light." Never a religion, it was a way of thinking akin to Unitarianism in that it rejected a belief in an arbitrary God and asserted the perfectability of all. It saw Deity as a pervading principle, to be found in all men everywhere. For the transcendentalist, revelation is supplanted by intuition, and man himself becomes the source of moral law. Those Unitarian intellectual leaders who developed their intuitive beliefs into a system, like Theodore Parker, were ostracized by orthodox Unitarians, who did not hold that God and the world are one, and that latently the soul of man contains all that the world contains. By its nature, transcendentalism as a doctrine meant just about what each individual exponent of it felt it to mean. Its disregard of external authority and logical demonstration, its belief that the self-reliant individual may better his nature through his own effort, its optimism — all are basic in the thought of William Ellery Channing the younger, Emerson, Thoreau, and George Ripley. Indeed, there was hardly a New

England writer of the time who remained untouched by its ideal-
istic philosophy.

The liberalism of Unitarians and transcendentalists was precisely the defection from a sound orthodoxy which the Valley deplored. The convictions which Emily Dickinson had inherited from
a Puritan past were still strongly held at home and enunciated
weekly in the pulpit of the First Church. They remained at the root
of all her thinking, though at times she thought she despised them.
But the governing influences in her day-by-day living were her
home and family rather than her reading. The winds of doctrine
blowing from Concord and Boston stirred her but did not greatly
affect her thinking. Her religious traditions held that man is a dependent creature whose intuitions are untrustworthy, that he is
not perfectible in this life or by his own effort, that he is not the
source of moral law, and that revelation is to be sought though it
cannot be guaranteed. These portions of the traditional orthodoxy —
and they constitute a major part of it — she clung to even in her
moments of severest doubt. Her philosophic utterances thus have a
durable consistency which they would lack had she expressed herself in terms of romantic idealism.

But her resentment against the dogmas in which she had been
trained crops up frequently. The doctrine of infant damnation she
found revolting, as did Oliver Wendell Holmes, who belonged to
her father's generation. She never became reconciled to the God
who punishes.

> Far from Love the Heavenly Father
> Leads the Chosen Child,
> Oftener through Realm of Briar
> Than the Meadow mild.
>
> Oftener by the Claw of Dragon
> Than the Hand of Friend
> Guides the Little One predestined
> To the Native Land.

The idea of a chosen few elected to salvation struck her as ridiculously exclusive. The poem beginning "How happy is the little Stone," ironically concludes that inanimateness alone can be "happy," because it alone fulfills absolute decree.

On one copy of it she vented her exasperation at the necessity for human limits by appending a note: "Heaven the Balm of a Surly Technicality!" One cannot be sure whether she thought the technicality by which one is predestined to salvation was imposed by theological orthodoxy or by the Deity. It is entirely possible that she was not sure herself, but one suspects that she is accusing the latter. When her nephew Gilbert was about six she sent him a verse that she titled "The Bumble Bee's Religion," bidding him carry it to his teacher. It is said to have accompanied a dead bee, and probably did.

> His little Hearse like Figure
> Unto itself a Dirge
> To a delusive Lilac
> The vanity divulge
> Of Industry and Morals
> And every righteous thing
> For the divine Perdition
> Of Idleness and Spring –

At the end she added, " 'All Liars shall have their part' – Jonathan Edwards – 'And let him that is athirst come' – Jesus." Emily Dickinson actually knew little about theology, and the unfairness to Edwards can be forgiven because her intent is to stress love, not punishment.

The sermons that she had heard expounded from the Valley pulpits more frequently expounded a jealous God than a compassionate Savior, and she became increasingly impatient with the doctrine of original sin, which as doctrine she mistakenly supposed, in common with most laymen and some divines, to mean a perverse disposition implanted at the time of conception rather than an inherent and necessary predisposition of all born into mortality. The extent to which her concept of *identity* parallels that of the philosopher Edwards will appear shortly. Edwards used it to explain "original sin." It is pertinent at the moment to say only that had Emily Dickinson been adequately acquainted with Edwards, she would have found that his view of the nature of man more nearly resembled her own than was true for most of her contemporaries.

To the extent that she thought about sin at all she associated it with the hypocrisy and timid conventions of "brittle" people who, like some Amherst ladies she knew, gave lip service to fair ideals, but had little love in their hearts.

> What soft – Cherubic Creatures –
> These Gentlewomen are –
> One would as soon assault a Plush –
> Or violate a Star –
>
> Such Dimity Convictions –
> A Horror so refined
> Of freckled Human Nature –
> Of Deity – ashamed –

When she wrote "The Bible is an antique Volume," she was thinking of the affirmations which make the precept to "love thy neighbor as thyself" so supreme. She was repelled by the decalogue of the "thou shalt nots." She concludes the poem:

> Sin – a distinguished Precipice
> Others must resist –
> Boys that 'believe' are very lonesome –
> Other Boys are 'lost'
> Had but the Tale a warbling Teller –
> All the Boys would come –
> Orpheus' Sermon captivated –
> It did not condemn –

The lines express precisely the thought of William Wordsworth, who said he'd rather be a pagan, suckled in a creed outworn, if he might have glimpses that would make him less forlorn.

Her gradual withdrawal from church attendance became absolute in her mid-twenties. For one so intensely religious by nature, such avoidance could not have been comfortable, and for Emily

Dickinson it set up stresses that are discernible throughout her life. Poetry she knew, if it made her feel physically as if the top of her head were taken off; and similarly she recognized preaching as an emotional experience. "He fumbles at your Soul," she wrote of preaching that had moved her, "As Players at the Keys." Then it:

> Deals – One – imperial – Thunderbolt –
> That scalps your Naked Soul –

What plagued her past endurance was the fact that men of the cloth, ministers trained to a professional knowledge of the mysteries, who themselves seemed to have mastered all doubts, could give no better answers to her questions than she already had found. Yet all her life she turned to them when her burdens seemed insupportable. They always responded willingly with a guidance that she never fully accepted. Ten months after the death in March 1853 of Ben Newton, the friend who had taught her immortality, she wrote to the pastor of Newton's church, Edward Everett Hale, to inquire whether Newton's last hours had been cheerful. "Please Sir, to tell me if he was willing to die, and if you think him at Home, I should love so much to know certainly that he was today in Heaven." A month after Wadsworth's death in April 1882, and long after she had apprehended all the answers any mortal could give her, she wrote Washington Gladden to inquire: "Is immortality true?" Gladden, whom she knew only as a distinguished clergyman, she singled out for inquiry because she still needed to discover, as all inquiring minds must do, whether another qualified searcher for truth had hit upon the formula that can relieve the ache of mystery. He answered that he could give no absolute demonstration, but averred that "a thousand lines of evidence converge toward it; and I believe it. It is all I can say." She had pushed him to limits that matched hers, and felt easier, one assumes, that his telescope pierced no further than her own.

The ministers of her church she treated with affectionate deference. When she learned the news of the resignation of the Reverend Jonathan Jenkins from the Amherst church to accept a call to the larger one in Pittsfield, she wrote banteringly: "We want you to conquer, but we want you to conquer here. 'Marathon is me.' Is there nothing but Glow in the new Horizon?"

The two men with whom she maintained an intimate correspondence for a quarter of a century were both ordained ministers. Though Higginson found even watered-down Unitarianism incompatible, and occupied no pulpit after 1861, Emily Dickinson knew his background, and that knowledge, certainly in part, shaped the nature of their preceptor-scholar relationship. Her very reasons for the long continued correspondence with Wadsworth, distinguished for his orthodoxy and for a pulpit manner which revealed to his congregations what Emily Dickinson called his "momentous nature," lay in the aid he must have given her in discussing points of doctrine. Her correspondence with Higginson is known, and it never directly touched upon spiritual matters. The nature of her letter exchange with Wadsworth is not known, but one imagines, in the light of her comment that he had been her shepherd "from 'little girl' hood," that she depended upon him for pastoral guidance.

The important question is: if Emily Dickinson found theological orthodoxies unacceptable, even repugnant, why did she turn in moments of greatest need to such men as Hale and Gladden and Wadsworth? Since so much of her poetry shows her kinship with the transcendentalists in their iconoclasm and distrust of institutions, why did she not find in the essays of George Ripley or the sermons of Theodore Parker, and especially in the persuasive voice of Emerson, all the affirmations that she needed? The answer is clear. Her "rapt attention" to immortality never deceived her senses into overlooking the essential difference between the nature of the Godhead and the nature of man. She knew that the immensity and obduracy of the Creator are beyond the grasp of the creature. Yet she was rebel enough not to accept willingly the limits that she knew are man's. She gave early expression to the thought in "Just lost – when I was saved." On the verge of finding the meaning of meaning she becomes "lost," in the sense of realizing that she will never discover it during her span of mortality.

She now began to record in poems each new awareness of her relation to the inscrutable. "This World is not Conclusion," she avers almost truculently, as though she hoped the assertion would forestall her own doubts; "And through a Riddle, at the last/ Sagacity must go." We have the witness of martyrs who have endured contempt and crucifixion for their faith, yet our uncertainty persists.

> Faith slips – and laughs, and rallies –
> Blushes, if any see –
> Plucks at a twig of Evidence –
> And asks a Vane, the way –
> Much Gesture, from the Pulpit –
> Strong Hallelujahs roll –
> Narcotics cannot still the Tooth
> That nibbles at the soul –

On occasion she queries whether simple stoicism may not be the answer. "Our journey had advanced," she imagines, to the fork in Being's road called Eternity.

> Before – were Cities – but Between –
> The Forest of the Dead –
>
> Retreat – was out of Hope –
> Behind – a Sealed Route –
> Eternity's White Flag – Before –
> And God – at every Gate –

Thus from the first she quested for certainties which from beginning to end she rejected. Yet in the light of her philosophic achievement in the years between 1862 and 1865, one can observe that the questings are directed less at her own uncertainties than at the gestures she saw and the hallelujahs she heard rolling from the Valley pulpits. She never again came near to matching the fecundity of those years, nor did she ever again deal so brilliantly with the philosophical problems now central in almost all the poems she was writing. A marked change occurs in the nature and the virtuosity of the poems written after she had made her adjustment to

Wadsworth's removal, and had undertaken, as it were, her preceptorial studies with Higginson. The lyrical, despairing outbursts of the bereaved bride come abruptly to an end. In their place she wrote a whole series of poems that establish her philosophical position on the nature and destiny of man. They are written with a serene detachment that shows the emergence of a new being.

Before looking at them, one must glance first at those she wrote about God as a person with whom, like Enoch of old, she was on friendliest terms. It was a relationship quite akin to that which Clarence Day's father maintained with God. She felt no hesitation in reminding God of his unfulfilled promises or bringing his attention to his own shortcomings. God had mistreated Moses by allowing the patriarch to view Canaan from Mount Pisgah but refusing entrance to him. Stephen and Paul had merely been put to death, while God's "adroiter" will

> On Moses – seemed to fasten
> With tantalizing Play
> As Boy – should deal with lesser Boy –
> To prove ability.

Reminding Mrs. Holland of the fact that Vinnie was her only sister, she comments: "God was penurious with me, which makes me shrewd with him." If God was sometimes a good banker or exchequer, he was also on occasion a marauding burglar, guilty of duplicity. "What did They do since I saw Them?" she ponders, having in mind the friends who have died. She would question them closely, if she could, so that only after the final question had been answered, "Should they start for the Sky."

> Not if Their Party were waiting,
> Not if to talk with Me
> Were to Them now, Homesickness
> After Eternity.
>
> Not if the Just suspect me
> And offer a Reward

IMMORTALITY

Would I restore my Booty
To that Bold Person, God –

She felt a liberty in speaking to God about such double-dealing that
she would never have presumed to take with any human friend. For
instance, what did God mean by creating man in his own image,
infinite in reason, only to return him to dust!

A Shade upon the mind there passes
As when on Noon
A Cloud the mighty Sun encloses
Remembering

That some there be too numb to notice
Oh God
Why give if Thou must take away
The Loved?

She jeers with mock politeness:

"Heavenly Father" – take to thee
The supreme iniquity
Fashioned by thy candid Hand
In a moment contraband –
Though to trust us – seems to us
More respectful – "We are Dust" –
We apologize to thee
For thine own Duplicity –

In a reminiscent mood she recalls that, when a child, she had
asked "Who are 'the Father and the Son,'" and says that had she
been able to learn, then "We better Friends had been, perhaps,"
because "Belief, it does not fit so well/ When altered frequently."
And she blushes to think that when she shall have achieved Heaven,
she will be ashamed to own it, having doubted it so often. She begins one poem "I never felt at Home – Below," and continues that
she won't feel at home in paradise "Because it's Sunday – all the
time/ And Recess – never comes."

If God could make a visit –
Or ever took a Nap –
So not to see us – but they say
Himself – a Telescope

Perennial beholds us –
Myself would run away
From Him – and Holy Ghost – and All –
But there's the "Judgment Day"!

The image of God as all-seeing is carried further in the poem that identifies consciousness with conscience, and the eye with burning lenses:

Of Consciousness, her awful Mate
The Soul cannot be rid –
As easy the secreting her
Behind the Eyes of God.

The deepest hid is sighted first
And scant to Him the Crowd –
What triple Lenses burn upon
The Escapade from God –

Her friend Maria Whitney had been slow in replying to a letter, and Emily wrote her: "You are like God. We pray to Him, and He answers 'No.' Then we pray to Him to rescind the 'No,' and he don't answer at all. Yet 'Seek and ye shall find' is the boon of faith." In verse she put it thus:

Of Course – I prayed –
And did God Care?
He cared as much as on the Air
A Bird – had stamped her foot –
And cried "Give Me" –

On one occasion she taunts God with being a distant, stately lover who woos the soul vicariously, like Myles Standish. But at other times he too was a boy, and therefore has fellow feeling. "Over the fence – Strawberries grow," she says, wishing she could pick them.

> But – if I stained my Apron –
> God would certainly scold!
> Oh dear – I guess if He were a Boy –
> He'd – climb – if He could!

There is winning intimacy in

> Papa above!
> Regard a Mouse
> O'erpowered by the Cat!
> Reserve within thy kingdom
> A "Mansion" for the Rat!

It was the very intimacy which she felt for the person of God that enabled her to engage in such banter. She was impatient with sacrosanct piety. "They are religious," she early wrote Higginson of her family," – except me – and address an Eclipse, every morning – whom they call their 'Father.'" And years later, writing to Helen Jackson after Mrs. Jackson had broken her leg, Emily Dickinson said in the same spirit: "Knew I how to pray, to intercede for your foot were intuitive, but I am a pagan." All this she could do because the person of God was a reality to her, and because God as a substance, in his transcendency, she knew worked from design. Observing the number of angleworms, "our little kinsmen," that appear as "a pink and pulpy multitude" after a rain, she ponders their usefulness.

> A needless life, it seemed to me
> Until a little Bird
> As to a Hospitality
> Advanced and breakfasted.

> As I of He, so God of Me
> I pondered, may have judged,
> And left the little Angle Worm
> With Modesties enlarged.

The unapproachable majesty of God as excellence is basic in her religious philosophy, and it is seen to run concurrently with her experience of God as a person. "My period had come for Prayer," she begins:

And so I stepped upon the North
To see this Curious Friend –

His House was not – no sign had He –
By Chimney – nor by Door
Could I infer his Residence –
Vast Prairies of Air

Unbroken by a Settler –
Were all that I could see –
Infinitude – Had'st Thou no Face
That I might look on Thee?

We may murmur against the creative will whose purpose is but the
"gambol of his authority,"

But His Perturbless Plan
Proceed – inserting Here – a Sun –
There – leaving out a Man –

Her concept of God as all-seeing, and as both light and glowing
heat, runs steadily through her verses.

The Sun and Moon must make their haste –
The Stars express around
For in the Zones of Paradise
The Lord alone is burned –

His Eye, it is the East and West –
The North and South when He
Do concentrate His Countenance
Like Glow Worms, flee away –

Oh Poor and Far –
Oh Hindered Eye
That hunted for the Day –
The Lord a Candle entertains
Entirely for Thee –

Among poets of the nineteenth century the romantic idea predominates that nature and God are one. Emily Dickinson is remark-

able in the degree to which her clear vision kept the Creator apart from the things created. Her Puritan heritage gave her a sense of reality in which pantheism has no place. The person capable of up-braiding God will not demean him by seeing him in a buttercup. Basically she conceived of God as infinitude, creative activity, mo-tion, light, incomprehensible immensity. His boundless sufficiency awed her but never made her cringe. His face is framed in circum-stances. The entire cosmos exists for his indwelling. Light and dark-ness are his acts when in his good time he wills them. All exist-ence serves or establishes his purpose. He remains hidden, a "Force illegible."

> All Circumstances are the Frame
> In which His Face is set –
> All Latitudes exist for His
> Sufficient Continent –
>
> The Light His Action, and the Dark
> The Leisure of His Will –
> In Him Existence serve or set
> A Force illegible.

The classic sublimity of the idea is matched by the eloquence of language. The word *set* is repeated, and the final word *illegible* is both unexpected and extraordinarily apt. The Force that she con-jures up is one that all can easily see but none can understand. The meaning is there surely, and in a language we know. Peer as we will, we simply cannot spell it out.

Emily Dickinson wrote comparatively few poems that deal with Christ as a person distinct from the Godhead. Her vision of Christ was almost entirely limited to his fellowship and humanity. The dialogue with Christ, written about 1864, is in the unpretentious language of everyday conversation:

> "Unto Me?" I do not know you –
> Where may be your House?
>
> "I am Jesus – Late of Judea –
> Now – of Paradise" –

Wagons – have you – to convey me?
This is far from Thence –

"Arms of Mine – sufficient Phaeton –
Trust Omnipotence" –

I am spotted – "I am Pardon" –
I am small – "The Least
Is esteemed in Heaven the Chiefest –
Occupy my House" –

In 1881 she sent Colonel Higginson lines that she titled "Christ's Birthday."

The Savior must have been
A docile Gentleman –
To come so far so cold a Day
For little Fellowmen –

The Road to Bethlehem
Since He and I were Boys
Was leveled, but for that twould be
A rugged billion Miles –

Here is clear implication of divine mediation, but the emphasis and the feeling in both are upon human association.

Of paramount importance to Emily Dickinson was the problem of one's own identity and integrity, and she began by considering the mystery of suffering. "I can wade grief," she begins one of the first on that theme, and concludes with the assertion that pain alone gives power; that men, stranded in mortality, learn through discipline that pain is supportable. Anodynes that deaden it dull our sense of values. It is the power to see truth, even the most painful, that supports man. At the level of human association, such experience teaches compassion. She develops the idea in some detail in "I measure every Grief I meet," wherein she wonders how different sufferings compare, and concludes:

To note the fashions – of the Cross –
And how they're mostly worn –

Still fascinated to presume
That Some – are like My Own –

At a more objective level she finds that

The hallowing of Pain
Like hallowing of Heaven,
Obtains at a corporeal cost –
The Summit is not given.

And that is because only full measures can pay the cost of reaching so high: "All – is the price of all." Again in 1864 the idea takes its final shape in one of her best utterances.

Experience is the Angled Road
Preferred against the Mind
By – Paradox – the Mind itself –
Presuming it to lead

Quite Opposite – How Complicate
The Discipline of Man –
Compelling Him to Choose Himself
His Preappointed Pain –

How does man win freedom from fear of himself or of the unknowable in all acts and relationships? Whereas such an artist as Melville, upon precisely the same quest, had in his youth moved restlessly round the globe, Emily Dickinson stood still and dissected the atom. For her as for Melville the quest was baffling, at times tormenting, and continued throughout a lifetime. For both the easy assertion was no answer. "Is immortality true"? was a question she could still phrase to Gladden near the end of her life, but he could not know when he replied to it that nearly twenty years before she had scaled the bleaknesses to a height not matched by his asseveration.

The "self" she variously designates in such terms as the "undiscovered continent," and the "indestructible estate." The solitudes of space, of the sea, even of death, she styles populous assemblies compared to "That polar privacy – a soul admitted to itself."

On a Columnar Self –
How ample to rely
In Tumult – or Extremity –
How good the Certainty

That Lever cannot pry –
And Wedge cannot divide
Conviction – That Granitic Base –
Though None be on our Side –

Here the "self" is one's integrity: the convictions we live by even though they isolate us from those we love. And she concludes:

Suffice Us – for a Crowd –
Ourself – and Rectitude –
And that Assembly – not far off
From furthest Spirit – God.

In this moment of deepest assurance about the rightness of her way of thinking and living, she and God are close associates.

The straight path to her seclusion she deliberately chose, the better to enable her to participate in the common experiences of all mankind. She had elected to do so in 1862, when her creativeness was at flood and she sensed that her fulfillment as artist required time to spend with the hosts that visited her. "The Soul selects her own Society," she said, "Then – shuts the door." She has in mind a way of life, and she will remain unmoved even though chariots pause at her low gate or an emperor kneels upon her mat, presumably to beg her to alter her convictions or to offer inducements for accepting other close associations.

I've known her – from an ample nation –
Choose One –
Then – close the Valves of her attention –
Like Stone –

The poem is universalized, but at the personal level it states her intent to live by her convictions.

The poem beginning "The Soul unto itself" deals with the

Hamlet theme, about which she never ceased to brood with acute sensitivity. The soul is either an "imperial friend" or the most "agonizing Spy." If it is secure against its own treachery, why should it fear that which is abroad?

> Itself – it's Sovreign – of itself
> The Soul should stand in Awe.

In "One need not be a Chamber – to be Haunted" the awe is spectral: "The Brain has Corridors – surpassing/ Material Place," she says, concluding that "Ourself behind ourself, concealed –/ Should startle most." This was the thought in her mind when she remarked to Colonel Higginson in 1873 that there is one thing to be grateful for: that one is oneself and not somebody else.

Especially charming are the poems which deal with the relationship between the soul and heaven, that is, between man's questing spirit and the manifestations in the world about us which uplift the spirit and surcharge it. The cordiality is that of host and guest. "The Soul should always stand ajar," so that if heaven (the guest) comes to call, the soul (the host) may be ready to welcome the ecstatic experience. The same relationship is envisioned in the poem that declares: "The Soul that hath a Guest/ Doth seldom go abroad," because "Diviner Crowd at Home –/ Obliterate the need."

> And Courtesy forbid
> A Host's departure when
> Upon Himself be visiting
> The Emperor of Men –

In yet another written during these years of serene detachment she expresses the thought in terms of limitless wealth. "To own the Art within the Soul" is like owning "an Estate perpetual/ Or a reduceless Mine." Nowhere is her artistic achievement more brilliantly fused with her deepened sense of destiny than in the four stanzas on the soul's identity. It is not an analysis of the relation of God and man, or of the relation of the soul to the body.

She is not talking about man as a being, who thus shares in history the consequences of human limits; or of man, the creature, subject to the biases of his nature. The poem attempts a most unusual feat: to analyze the naked soul itself. It does so with an extraordinary combination of emotional detachment and inward vision. We who are conscious today of the world about us, she says, on occasion may become aware that we are experiencing an interval between the immortality whence we came and whither we will return. Such consciousness is uniquely the property of each individual. A man's soul is an identity that can never be known to others or shared by them. The adventure of living, wherein our souls are placed in mortal frames, condemns us to solitude. The truth is that though men, as creatures, share destinies in common, man as the steward of his soul is profoundly isolated. We are born alone, and alone do we die. But the important thing is that, change as we may inwardly or outwardly over the years, our identities endure. Identity is thus perception, idea, and an act of God.

> This Consciousness that is aware
> Of Neighbors and the Sun
> Will be the one aware of Death
> And that itself alone
>
> Is traversing the interval
> Experience between
> And most profound experiment
> Appointed unto Men —
>
> How adequate unto itself
> It's properties shall be
> Itself unto itself and none
> Shall make discovery.
>
> Adventure most unto itself
> The Soul condemned to be —
> Attended by a single Hound
> It's own identity.

The microcosm of her identity, she implies, is a prototype of all identities, made one by the fact of like properties and qualities. The observation itself is profound, and is precisely the concept of identity set forth by Jonathan Edwards in his "Notes on the Mind," and in his argument which finds in sin the oneness of mankind. It may not have occurred to Emily Dickinson that in this poem of fewer than seventy words she performed a feat that volumes of theological exegesis have never made so immediate to apprehension. In art form she has depicted ultimate reality: the working of the Holy Spirit. We return to it for contemplation as we do to Michelangelo's Judgment and Verdi's Requiem.

The evidences of emotional intensity, displayed in her inability to meet people, grew acutely with the years after 1870. Though she thereafter wrote comparatively fewer poems, she lived intimately in her correspondence, on which she lavished great care. But in the early sixties, the years of full creativeness when she was working out her testament on the nature and destiny of man, she was less concerned about her outside relationships and therefore able to give scope to the themes that absorbed her. It was during these years that she moved on to deal with two further and, for her, final problems of immortality: the theme of eternity and the theme of the love of God. On these matters she had no doubts whatsoever. Her best poems on these subjects, in fact nearly all that she wrote on them, were set down in the four years 1862–1865. The first line of one of the 1862 poems is witness to her belief about eternity.

> Forever – is composed of Nows –
> Tis not a different time –
> Except for Infiniteness –
> And Latitude of Home –

That lays the groundwork. In the same year she builds further.

> Heaven is so far of the Mind
> That were the Mind dissolved –
> The Site – of it – by Architect
> Could not again be proved

'Tis vast – as our Capacity –
As fair – as our idea –
To Him of adequate desire
No further 'tis, than Here –

Eternity is at once both of and outside of time. Furthermore, like identity, it is idea. In fact, she perceived, it is identity.

The Blunder is in estimate.
Eternity is there
We say as of a Station.
Meanwhile he is so near
He joins me in my Ramble –
Divides abode with me –
No Friend have I that so persists
As this Eternity.

Eternity is personified, or at least animated, as is the single hound "identity." It is a close friend whether at home or abroad on a ramble. Eternity is in fact the animus: that part of her, call it mind, idea, identity, which makes her one with all the rest of humanity, whether as persons they have long since passed from existence or are yet to be born. Though no autograph copy of the poem survives, the manner in which the ideas unfold places it in those years when her affirmations were taking shape.

All these utterances are her way of expressing the profoundly simple truth that the kingdom of heaven is within. How easily even the best-intentioned people can forfeit salvation if the heart falters or is misdirected!

Not probable – The barest Chance –
A smile too few – a word too much
And far from Heaven as the Rest –
The Soul so close on Paradise –

What if the Bird from journey far –
Confused by Sweets – as Mortals – are –
Forget the secret of His wing

And perish – but a Bough between –
Oh, Groping feet –
Oh Phantom Queen!

The union with Christ is represented in terms which all Puritans would have understood, and draws upon the metaphor of marriage ("Queen") in the manner of the Song of Solomon, a book of the Bible especially cherished in New England. The experience carries over into one of her love poems, "I live with Him," written about the same time in 1862, concluding:

I live with Him – I hear His Voice –
I stand alive – Today –
To witness to the Certainty
Of Immortality –

Taught Me – by Time – the lower Way –
Conviction – Every day –
That Life like This – is stopless –
Be Judgment – what it may.

This poem likewise gives time a dual function. It is here and now, passing slowly with the tick of the clock. It is also eternal. The "lower" way is the tick-of-the-clock waiting, in mortality, for the perpetual union which the beating heart in sensation intuitively feels to be "stopless."

One of her last poems on the subject of immortality, written about 1874, is a noble poetic utterance. The quick but unhurried measure of the Short Meter is combined with exact rhyme. The assurance of the words is matched by that of the form in which they are expressed.

Two Lengths has every Day –
It's absolute extent
And Area superior
By Hope or Horror lent –

Eternity will be
Velocity or Pause

At Fundamental Signals
From Fundamental Laws –

To die is not to go –
On Doom's consummate Chart
No Territory new is staked –
Remain thou as thou art.

Here is no mystical, transcendental identification with the divine, but rather an echo of the trumpet voice of the seers and prophets, who speak not visions only, but a judgment: identity cannot be lost.

In dealing with her final theme, the love of God, Emily Dickinson went beyond theological orthodoxy. One observes how she felt that eternity is tied into love now, yesterday, and always. All immortality for her was a quality of spirit, a vital force, to be recognized in this life. She wrote Samuel Bowles, whose integrity she felt matched his zest for living: "You have the most triumphant face out of Paradise, probably because you are there constantly, instead of ultimately"; and after his death in 1878 she phrased the thought again to Mary Bowles: "As he was himself Eden, he is with Eden, for we cannot become what we were not." This sense of intimacy with the everlasting she strikingly expressed again to Mary Bowles two years later: "Immortality as a guest is sacred, but when it becomes as with you and with us, a member of the family, the tie is more vivid." She is thinking of the fact that both her father and "Mr. Sam" are dead and, she likes to think, enjoying paradise together, but she is signifying her belief that immortality, as all love must, begins at home. It is, she says, a way of life that can be elected. "Paradise is of the option," she once wrote Colonel Higginson. "Whosoever will – own Eden notwithstanding Adam and Repeal." She carried the thought forward with a penetration which her friends among the clergy must have found exhilarating, even though they could not theologically have supported it. In her letter of condolence to Colonel Higginson after the death of his wife Mary Channing Higginson, she said: "To be human is more than to be divine, for when Christ was divine, he was uncontented till he had been human."

She has gone beyond all Christian orthodoxies by conferring upon the creature a partnership with the Creator. She insists that love is meaningless unless it is reciprocated, both in this life and in the life to come; and that God himself is not yet perfected, and perhaps never will be. Man of course is totally dependent upon God, but in some way, to some degree, God needs the love of man to keep the cycles wheeling and the stars in their course. To this extent Jehovah for her is not Zeus, all-sufficient, infallible, and arbitrary; but Prometheus, the friend of mankind, capable of suffering. She has also in mind the love which St. Paul talks about as the possession of all men who search their own hearts to find it: "Love is it's own rescue," she continues in her letter to Higginson, "for we – at our supremest, are but it's trembling Emblems." "My Faith is larger than the Hills," she declares, because it endures beyond the phenomena of nature.

> So when the Hills decay –
> My Faith must take the Purple Wheel
> To show the Sun the way –

And she concludes:

> How dare I, therefore, stint a faith
> On which so vast depends –
> Lest Firmament should fail for me –
> The Rivet in the Bands.

This concept of man as the rivet, whose love thereby allows God to achieve fulfillment, suggests a four-dimensional concept of the universe wherein all elements are interdependent. It throws clear light upon the nature of her skepticism. To have less faith in the upward striving creature than in the outstretched arm of the Creator, she says here and often elsewhere, is to expect a less than perfect union between God and man. Viewed in this light, her query many years later "Is immortality true?" was only a way of asking whether the theological concept of an arbitrary and self-sufficient deity did in fact get at the whole truth.

> As plan for Noon and plan for Night
> So differ Life and Death
> In positive Prospective –
> The Foot upon the Earth
>
> At Distance, and Achievement, strains,
> The Foot upon the Grave
> Makes effort at conclusion
> Assisted faint of Love.

The same ringing assurance appears in such poems as "Faith – is the Pierless Bridge," "I never saw a moor," and "Split the Lark – and you'll find the Music" — the last with its taunt at those who would classify the unknowable:

> Scarlet Experiment! Sceptic Thomas!
> Now, do you doubt that your Bird was true?

There is Promethean rebelliousness in such poems as "Bind me – I still can sing." The will to share burns insistently in a large number of the poems written during this cycle.

> So large my Will
> The little that I may
> Embarrasses
> Like gentle infamy –
>
> Affront to Him
> For whom the Whole were small
> Affront to me
> Who know His Meed of all.
>
> Earth at the best
> Is but a scanty Toy –
> Bought, carried Home
> To Immortality.
>
> It looks so small
> We chiefly wonder then

At our Conceit
In purchasing.

At the same time her love poems strengthened and universalized.

Love – is anterior to Life –
Posterior – to Death –
Initial of Creation, and
The Exponent of Earth –

Love and death, both components of immortality here, share and are shared. In "Behind Me – dips Eternity" she conceives of herself as "the Term between" it and the immortality ahead. Here death is:

. . . but the Drift of Eastern Gray,
Dissolving into Dawn away,
Before the West begin –

Her profoundest insights focus in the poem "The Admirations – and Contempts of Time," which she says, "Show justest – through an Open Tomb." The fact of dying "Reorganizes Estimate," so that we have, as it were,

Compound Vision –
Light – enabling Light –
The Finite – furnished
With the Infinite –
Convex – and Concave Witness –
Back – toward Time –
And forward –
Toward the God of Him –

Love, faith, death, immortality – the four dimensions – are the forces by which the willing creature is bound to the willing God. Her currents here flow into all subterranean oceans. The search for the meaning of love could take her this far in 1864:

Till Death – is narrow Loving –
The scantest Heart extant

Will hold you till your privilege
Of Finiteness – be spent –

But He whose loss procures you
Such Destitution that
Your Life too abject for itself
Thenceforward imitate –

Until – Resemblance perfect –
Yourself, for His pursuit
Delight of Nature – abdicate –
Exhibit Love – somewhat –

Love goes infinitely beyond the grave, and we become better images of those we loved because we try to imitate them. Thus are we made willing to die.

> Unable are the Loved to die
> For Love is Immortality
> Nay, it is Deity –

Her muse has led her to the discovery of secret springs in her own desert.

The skilful portraiture of aspects of nature lie ahead; a thunderstorm, sunset, or pebble; a cricket, hummingbird, or oriole. Some of them are among the first order of nature lyrics, and they typify the deepened sympathies now rechanneled for the most part into her voluminous correspondence. They were written during the last fifteen years of her life when her outward activities, so far as they could be observed by neighbors, seemed confined to caring for her invalid mother, tending her flowers, and enjoying the association of small children. The few friends who knew her well were aware of the inner activity which never abated. But her philosophic testament had been written by 1865. Her first interest, "circumference," would be her last. In 1864 she could express her sense of immortality with classic restraint:

> Ample make this Bed
> Make this Bed with Awe

IMMORTALITY

In it wait till Judgment break
Excellent and Fair

Be it's Mattrass straight
Be it's Pillow round
Let no Sunrise' Yellow noise
Interrupt this Ground.

Twenty years later, ill and measuring the weeks of her own distance from awe and circumference, she could write this stave:

Back from the cordial Grave I drag thee
He shall not take thy Hand
Nor put his spacious arm around thee
That none can understand

Prometheus to the last, she wishes to participate with amplitude
in the limits that are universal.

CHRONOLOGY

BIBLIOGRAPHICAL NOTE

INDEXES

IMPORTANT DATES IN THE LIFE OF EMILY DICKINSON

1828 Edward Dickinson, of Amherst, married Emily Norcross, of Monson, 6 May

1829 William Austin Dickinson (brother), born 16 April

1830 Emily Elizabeth Dickinson, born 10 December

1833 Lavinia Norcross Dickinson (sister), born 28 February

1840 Dickinson family moved from the Main Street homestead into a house on Pleasant Street
Portraits of the three children, and of the parents, painted by O. A. Bullard

1844 Emily visited relatives in Boston, Cambridge, and Worcester during May and June. She visited in Boston also in 1846 and 1851

1847 She graduated from Amherst Academy after six years of irregular attendance

1847–1848 She attended Mount Holyoke Female Seminary, at South Hadley

1850 Earliest publication: prose valentine in Amherst undergraduate magazine *The Indicator*

1852 First published poem: "Sic transit gloria mundi," (titled "A Valentine"), in *Springfield Daily Republican*, 20 February
Edward Dickinson elected to Congress

1854 Dickinson family visited in Washington and Philadelphia, April and May

1855 Dickinson family moved back to the homestead

1856 Austin Dickinson and Susan Gilbert married, 1 July

1858 Emily began to assemble fair copies of her poems

1860 Charles Wadsworth called on Emily, early in the year

1861 "I taste a liquor never brewed," (titled "The May-Wine"), in *Springfield Daily Republican,* 4 May

Edward (Ned) Dickinson, son of Austin and Susan, born 19 June

1862 "Safe in their alabaster chambers" (titled "The Sleeping"), in *Springfield Daily Republican,* 1 March

Charles Wadsworth accepts call to Calvary Church in San Francisco; acceptance announced, 15 March

Samuel Bowles goes to Europe for his health, 9 April

Emily initiates correspondence about her poetry with Thomas Wentworth Higginson, 15 April

1864 Lavinia Dickinson takes her sister to Boston for an eye examination, February

"Some keep the sabbath going to church" (titled "My Sabbath"), in *The Round Table,* 12 March

"Blazing in gold and quenching in purple" (titled "Sunset"), in *Springfield Daily Republican,* 30 March

Emily is in Boston (sojourning with her nieces in Cambridge) for eye treatment, April–November

1865 Eye treatment renewed, April–October

1866 "A narrow fellow in the grass" (titled "The Snake"), in *Springfield Daily Republican,* 14 February

Martha Gilbert Dickinson, daughter of Austin and Susan, born 30 November

1867–1868 The two least documented years of Emily Dickinson's life

1869 Charles Wadsworth returned to Philadelphia

1870 Higginson paid his first visit, 16 August

1873 Higginson paid his second (last) visit, 3 December

1874 Edward Dickinson (father) died, 16 June

1875 Emily's mother paralyzed, June

Thomas Gilbert Dickinson, the son of Austin and Susan, born 1 August

1876 Helen Hunt Jackson called, 10 October

1878 Samuel Bowles died, 16 January

Helen Hunt Jackson called a second time, with her husband, 24 October

"Success," in *A Masque of Poets,* November

CHRONOLOGY

1880 Charles Wadsworth called, during the summer

1881 Josiah Gilbert Holland died, 12 October

1882 Charles Wadsworth died, 1 April
     Emily's mother died, 14 November

1883 Gilbert Dickinson died, 5 October

1884 Otis P. Lord died, 13 March
     Emily suffered a nervous collapse, 14 June

1885 Helen Hunt Jackson died, 12 August
     Emily's own illness severe in November

1886 Emily Dickinson died, 15 May

BIBLIOGRAPHICAL NOTE

THE TEXTS of all Dickinson poems, and of all letters quoted herein, derive from autographs if such are known to exist. The text of the poems follows that in *The Poems of Emily Dickinson* (Cambridge: Harvard), 1955. All excerpts from letters, whether published or unpublished, are used by the kind permission of the owners and copyright owners where copyright exists. The poems and excerpts of poems still in copyright under the control of Houghton Mifflin & Company and of Little, Brown & Company are reproduced by their kindness.

The letters to Jane Humphrey, all privately owned, are unpublished. All letters to Thomas Wentworth Higginson are in *Letters of Emily Dickinson,* edited by Mabel Loomis Todd (second edition, New York: Harper), 1931. The text in this biography derives from the autographs in the Boston Public Library. Higginson's diaries are in Harvard College Library, as is one letter noted in Chapter VIII, but his notes written after meeting Emily Dickinson are in the Boston Public Library. All Holland letters are in *Emily Dickinson's Letters to Dr. and Mrs. Josiah Gilbert Holland,* edited by Theodora Van Wagenen Ward (Cambridge: Harvard), 1951. The autographs are in Harvard College Library. Autographs of letters to Louise and Frances Norcross do not survive; the text derives from *Letters.* Unless otherwise noted below, the letters to Abiah Root are unpublished and are in Harvard College Library; so likewise are the letters of Helen Hunt Jackson and Thomas Niles to Emily Dickinson.

CHAPTER I. Letters exchanged between members of the Dickinson and Norcross families (pages 5, 11) are in Harvard College Library and are unpublished, as are the letters to Susan Gilbert (pages 17–18). Excerpts from the letters to Abiah Root on pages 13, 14, 16 are derived from *Letters* (ed. 1931), pages 28–29, 34, 49. The quotations from letters to Susan Gilbert (page 16) derive from autographs in Harvard

College Library; the letters are published in *Emily Dickinson Face to Face* (Boston: Houghton Mifflin), 1932, edited by Martha Dickinson Bianchi.

CHAPTER II. The letters to Austin and Lavinia Dickinson (pages 23–24, 34) are in Harvard College Library, and are unpublished. The letter to Mrs. Haven, in Harvard College Library, is published in *Indiana Quarterly for Bookmen*, I (1945), 116. The letters to Susan Gilbert Dickinson (pages 39–40, 43–44) are published in *Emily Dickinson Face to Face*. The excerpts from other letters to Austin Dickinson, to the Norcrosses, and to Mrs. Bowles, derive from *Letters* (ed. 1931).

CHAPTER III. The excerpts from three letters to Samuel Bowles (pages 45 and 47) derive from *Letters*; the longer excerpt to him (pages 47–48) is from a letter privately owned (Mr. Richard Hooker), and is unpublished. The sentence to Susan Dickinson (page 47) is from a letter in Harvard College Library, published in part in *The Life and Letters of Emily Dickinson* (Boston: Houghton Mifflin), 1924, edited by Martha Dickinson Bianchi. Drafts of letters to Judge Lord are in *Emily Dickinson: A Revelation* (New York: Harper), 1954, edited by Millicent Todd Bingham. The letter from Samuel Bowles to Austin Dickinson is in Harvard College Library, and is unpublished.

CHAPTER IV. The excerpts from letters to Austin Dickinson derive from *Letters*; the excerpt from the letter to E. E. Hale is from an autograph privately owned (Mr. Josiah K. Lilly); it is published in George F. Whicher, *This Was a Poet* (New York: Scribner), 1939, pages 84–85. The excerpt from the letter written by Higginson to Mrs. Todd (page 99) is quoted from Millicent Todd Bingham, *Ancestors' Brocades: The Literary Debut of Emily Dickinson* (New York: Harper), 1945, page 127.

CHAPTER V. The letter from Higginson to Emily Dickinson (pages 125–126) is in Harvard College Library, and is unpublished, as is the comment from Susan Dickinson (page 117). The letter to Mrs. Currier (page 132) is in *Letters*; the text derives from the autograph in Yale University Library.

CHAPTER VI. The letter to Daniel Chester French is lost. The text derives from a transcript kindly supplied by his daughter, Mrs. William Penn Cresson. In garbled form, and with the attached poem missing, it is published in *Emily Dickinson Face to Face*.

CHAPTER VII. Part of the letter from Mrs. Jackson to Emily Dickinson on page 177 is published in the preface to *Poems, Second Series* (1891). The excerpts of letters exchanged between Mrs. Todd and Higginson, and Higginson and Niles (pages 159 and 176), are derived from *Ancestors' Brocades*, pages 54, 82, and 237. The excerpt from the draft of a letter from Emily Dickinson to an unknown correspondent also derives from *Ancestors' Brocades*, page 84, and the quotation from Mrs. Todd's journal from page 166. Emily Dickinson's letters to Thomas Niles, to Maria Whitney, and to an unknown recipient (probably Mr. Jackson), are in *Letters*.

CHAPTER VIII. The letter to Higginson (pages 195–196) is in Harvard College Library.

CHAPTER X. The letter to Hale is the one quoted in Chapter IV.

INDEX OF POEMS

INDEX

INDEX

GENERAL INDEX